Alight

Alight

**Alight the train
of thoughts and stories about yourself
and start living as the light that you are**

Lisette Schuitemaker

Lisette Schuitemaker
Alight

Published by Eos

ISBN 978-0-9892289-8-5

Printed and Bound in the United States

EOS

For who we really are.

a•light [1] (ə-līt')

itr.v. **a•light•ed** or **a•lit** (ə-lĭt'), **a•light•ing**, **a•lights**

1. To come down and settle, as after flight: *a sparrow alighting on a branch.*

2. To get down, as from a vehicle; dismount: *The queen alighted from the carriage.*

3. To come by chance: *alight on a happy solution.*

Proposal to thefreedictionary.com:

4. To realize each of us is a light, part of the all light.

Contents

FRONTLIGHT

U pon birth we first see the light of day. What we bring with us already is the light that we are; the light of life that is invisible to the naked eye and that is unbreakably connected with all light; light that is indivisible, always one and the same no matter in how many different forms and shapes it shows itself to us. We are light. Light materializing as the unique one that we are.

Consider for a moment the water flowing in our rivers and streams. The drops that form these waterways do not belong to any one or anything. Depending on where we live, we might call the Amazon, Mississippi, Nile, Rhine, Thames or Yangtse our river. When we do, we name the banks that hold the flow rather than the water itself. The water springs from a source somewhere or comes down from snowy mountaintops on its inevitable way to the ocean or the sea. The water in oceans, seas, lakes, rivers, canals, streams, ponds, puddles, pipes, taps, tubs and cups everywhere is one water. In one place it evaporates into clouds that float their own way to come down as rain somewhere else. Every drop of water is connected to all water on our planet. It is all one water, really.

The same goes for light. There is light. Not one light. Light. Indivisible, inexhaustible, invincible light. It does not belong to a person, an organization or a state. Light is. It is always connected with itself and in itself. All light is one. It travels through the universe at dazzling speed and brings us to life. The light. You are made of it. You are a light. Whatever your life circumstances, however you may feel inwardly at this point in time, you are and will always be light. We are all manifestations of the one light. The all-light. A light at the time.

All Alight

In the spring of 2009, I was traveling from Amsterdam to London by train. Through Belgium into the northern part of France, through the Chunnel and you're there before you know it. Upon arrival we were requested by the polite British staff to alight the train as it had reached its final destination. I remember being struck by this sentence. To alight the train – what a lovely happy-making expression! The word-lover in me immediately saw potential for its usage way beyond the British railways. Worldwide people could start to remind themselves to alight the train of their thoughts and stories about themselves and know themselves again as the light that they are. A light. We are all a light. Part of the one light. That is how this book got started.

I pay homage to the Brits for keeping this word alive even after it has left the normal vocabulary. And here and now I start a campaign to bring this verb back into usage. Just say it out loud a few times, taste it on the tip of your tongue: alight. Do you notice how your spirit is lifted? Do you sit just a bit more upright than a moment ago? When we speak its name, the light in us responds straight away. We lighten up whenever we invoke the light that is at the core of our being. Say it three times inwardly and you will feel lighter instantaneously. Whisper alight as if you impart a secret to a child and sense the tenderness in your being. Shout it out loud in the privacy of your bedroom and feel instantly empowered. It works like magic. Just give it a try. Say alight to yourself when you go out the door. Start being an alighter and you will soon find yourself a lighter being. You'll start to see open windows where once you assumed closed doors. That is what this book is about.

Invoking the light is an antidote to the fast forgetting that happens to all of us. Before we know it, our thoughts take us for a ride and we think what we've always thought and thus end up in the same old, same old. We forget to alight our train of thoughts and realize that we are light already. Especially when we are having a hard time, we are prone to lose contact with who we truly are. We contract and once in the downward spiral we lose sight of who we are and what we are capable of. We get lost in the jumbly jungle of our thoughts, emotions and expectations. We reduce ourselves to zero and soon start to feel lonely, alone and misunderstood.

To counter the great forgetting we must do perpetual maintenance. In the Netherlands, where I live below sea level as many of us do, our coastlines are slowly eaten away by the sea. So we need to do perpetual maintenance and restore the dunes and dikes constantly in order to be able to live behind them. In other places on earth, the desert expands unless the soil is retained by the roots of trees and plants. As humans, wherever we live, we must be vigilant to counter the persisting erosion of the forgetting we are all prone to.

Alight. Do you feel what happens just reading that word? Isn't it amazing how quickly something in you lightens up, like a lamp switching on and suddenly brightening the space? Do the corners of your mouth curl up? Do you notice a change in your glance, the way you might look at the world with just a touch more compassion? Do you feel your heart opening wider? Are you aware, maybe, of emitting light as if you were a lightbulb switched on? Feeling this way is yours for the taking. Anytime. Just alight.

Lightening Up

In the past thirty years, I have talked to hundreds of people. As a journalist for magazines and an interviewer for corporations while I had my own communication agency, as a board member for foundations and other organizations that work for a world of unity, and as a healer, coach, friend, aunt and woman in general. My approach has always been not to prepare a conversation but to prepare myself for the conversation. For an interview, for example, I would never come with a list of questions prepared beforehand. I would read the available information and then trust that the right questions would pop up in me and that I would be able to conduct a conversation in such a way that it became an inspiring co-creation. Except for once, early in my career. I had to interview a high-level banker who had the reputation of not suffering fools lightly. I came with a list of well-researched questions. He looked right through me.

"I know where that comes from – a rubbish newspaper article!"

I felt like a fool. Then he laughed out loud and I was able to let go of my premeditated action. Away with my list. On to true contact. And so we let our light shine together on what he had to say and I had to ask. This incidence confirmed to me that we can fully trust that we have all we need with us always already. Of course, one can prepare but then you need to let go. And trust. I am a light, part of the all light. And so are you. We all are. If we can allow the light in us to connect to the light in the other, we can be open to what wants to happen between us. We can co-create.

To be able to do so requires an inner attitude that I describe here with three qualifications. To be able to co-create with life as part of life one needs to be *lightfooted*. Can you dance with what arises in the moment whatever it is? That's what life wants to know. It requires us to be *lightheaded*. In other words that we don't let images from our past or future color our observation of what happens now. Can we be empty and open at all times to see what arises in the moment? And it wants us to be *lighthearted*. This means that we are able to remain true to our deepest calling and play the role that is uniquely ours to play. Alighting the train of our conditionings, patterns and thoughts, we can know ourselves as light. A light part of all light. And start to live a light-emitting life.

Three Thick Curtains

Light connects to light instantly. As I sit here writing, I am burning a candle. It is in no competition with the light that floods in through the window. It has a different quality, each to their own. Light is not competitive. It is. Yet, when it comes to ourselves and the light that enlivens us, there is a persistent thought that tells us we'd better not let our light shine too brightly. We might embarrass ourselves or outshine another and you don't want that to happen, do you? So somewhere early in our lives we start to hide our light. Just to be safe. And as is often the case, what we think is going to keep us safe in actual fact hampers our full expression.

I have had the privilege of working with lots of people in the past ten years, who wanted to get more out of life and out of themselves. They wanted to love again, shine once more in their profession, turn their hobby into their work, take a step into the unknown, accept the support of others, find their way out of depression or retrace their steps to their partner. Whatever they came in with, in a certain sense all their issues boiled down to one and the same thing. At some point they had pulled a curtain; closed off a part of themselves; curtailed themselves by keeping part of their uniqueness safely hidden. Learning by doing I discovered the Three Thick Curtains. In each of the upcoming chapters I describe such a curtain and show you how you can open it so the light can shine in again and you can let your full light shine brightly.

The Curtain of the Painstake

Each time that you think or say: "Yes, but if I were to do that, then ..." you close the Curtain of the Painstake a little further. This ubiquitous phrase seems to imply that you will not fare well if you were to take the action. Is that really so? In chapter 1 we will take a closer look at how you have painstakingly kept parts of yourself hidden. Sharing stories and examples I will show you the trap of the Painstake that we keep ourselves locked in without knowing it. Once you are aware of this trap, you can free yourself in three simple steps. Behind the Curtain of the Painstake lies a world of lightfootedness.

The Curtain of the Many Stories

A human being is like a book with volumes and volumes of stories that we like to tell each other. But beware: a story of your life is not your life. If you tell a story too often, it becomes a groove that you can get stuck in. Also, there is the very human tendency to depict ourselves just a little bit better than is the case. The other person was out of their mind and we, of course, were right. Each time that you beautify a story for your own benefit, you pull the Curtain of the Many Stories closer. In chapter 2 you will find a parable that shows how beautifying our stories hides our light. And what three exercises you can do to avoid the trap of the great forgetting. This leads to *lightheaded* living.

The Curtain of the Critical Voice-over

If we were to talk to family and friends in the tone we sometimes use to get ourselves in shape, we would soon have no one left. What is behind this critical inner voice-over who seems to be able to find fault with whatever we do? This you discover in chapter 3. Here, too, you will find three consecutive steps to help you find the meaning of your life and turn the discontented voice-over into a constructive ally. So that you can act meaningfully in the world. So that you can be *lighthearted*.

Three Light Life Approaches

On the other side of these three thick curtains is a world to be won. In the examples that I share in this book you will see that we have always had a reason to fence a part of ourselves off – to hide bits of ourselves behind inner smokescreens. The question is: does the reason we chose to hide still hold true now that we have grown up? Does this habit serve us or dis-serve us now that we are adults? Do the inner curtains prevent us from letting our light shine? If so, that as a non-registered believer I believe is sin. We are meant to shine. For those who have plucked up the courage to look behind the thick curtains, there is a huge reward. Life-size. As the light that you already are, always have been and always will be, you will experience and conduct yourself in these ways:

Lightfooted

When you no longer let yourself be limited by what others might think of you; when you step out of the Painstake that holds you often without you being aware of it, then you will naturally become light on your feet. You will dance with life and with whatever situation it presents you with.

Lightheaded

Creation creates all the time. It cannot help itself. Lightheaded living is to be able to be fully in the moment. And in doing so co-create with what wants to happen. This requires you to hold your habit of catching your life in stories against the light. A story keeps you stuck like a needle in a groove while life is forever moving.

Lighthearted

The meaning of your life is your life itself. To experience this is to live in a lighthearted way. You will perceive your life as meaningful, because you do what only you can do. From moment to moment you choose to take the risk that your actions will not be understood or your love will not be seen. Yet you do what you do as it is yours to do. And because deep inside you have full faith in the light that shines through no one exactly the way it does through you.

New Language

On the pages that follow you will meet lots of people who in these past years have made me privy to their life questions. I share conversations that I had with clients, colleagues, friends and family. Their names and situations I have changed so they can recognize themselves whilst remaining anonymous to others. Sometimes I have combined various people into one. And I also describe how I put my theories to practice in my own life.

Writing is playing with words. Long ago I studied the Classics with a major in Latin. I was in search of the source of our civilization, our judicial system, our way of thinking. As a bonus of reading and translating two-thousand year old texts I developed a deep love for how words are composed. I like to take a peek into words, take them apart and find new meanings. Alight is an example. In the course of this book, I propose new meanings for words that have light in them. For the usual meaning I have consulted thefreedictionary.com and, as you will see, I have some recommendations.

Lighters

Here and there I give practical tips for how to conduct a conversation with yourself or someone else lightly. These tips are marked like this:

light•er 1 (lī'tər) n.

1. One that ignites or kindles.

2. A mechanical device for lighting a cigarette, cigar, or pipe.

Proposal to thefreedictionary.com:

3. The inner capacity to live as the light that we all are and as such emit light naturally.

LIGHTFOOTED

light-foot•ed (līt'foot'ĭd) also **light•foot** (-foot') adj.

1. Treading with light and nimble ease.

Proposal to thefreedictionary.com:

2. Being able to move beyond painstakingly adhering to what is usual and thus see more ways than one to bake a cake.

B eing able to dance with life. That is lightfooted living. It is being quick and versatile, ever searching and seeing openings and options, moving through life elegantly, nimble on your feet. Realizing, feeling, knowing that you are already a light and thus are never ever separate or alone. The light that you are is always connected to all light. Alight.

Lightfooted people are problem solvers. Where others see an obstacle, they find the angle that make issues stand in a new light. Where another would let themselves be limited by what others might think, the lightfooted one walks their own creative path. Where some are inclined to give up, they see a chance.

This does not mean that lightfooted people are superficial. They just make the choice not to take the heavy road but travel the light one instead. They opt for the approach that can bring lightness by being a sunny presence. They bring light also to places of deep darkness.

One finds lightfooted people everywhere; in all countries, in all strata of society. They move with life. Like the woman in the flower shop who happily writes her account number on the wrapping of my beautiful bouquet when I discover I have left my wallet on the kitchen table. Of course, I can take the flowers home. Trust rules here. That is lightfooted living. Or someone like Kofi Annan who, as Secretary General of the United Nations, had a knack for coming up with original proposals for issues long given up by all. They are people who are able to do the unusual, original, never done before and yet perfectly fitted to the moment and the occasion at hand.

The Curtain of the Painstake

Why are we often rather heavy-hearted than lightfooted? Ah, that is the school of life. You start out being spontaneous. Someone has a criticism on something you did and you take fright. Or you get no response at all to something you did out of love. We all suffer these kinds of situations and one day when we are young we draw the conclusion that we'd better not do what we did anymore. We start to observe what is desired behavior and we adapt. Before we know it we uphold all kinds of rules of conduct the way we understood them as a young child. Since we do not want to run the risk of losing the love of our dear ones, we painstakingly adhere to what someday seemed right.

No one comes fully unharmed out of youth. Somewhere along the way we have all fenced off, suppressed or swallowed parts of ourself. The beauty is that at any given age you can still learn to trust your own intuition; to not mind so much what another might think; to take life lightly.

"Yes, but if I were to do that, then …"

Yes, then what? The answer to that question is the subject of our inquiry in this chapter. The stories and examples I give will make you see the trap that I call the painstake that we unconsciously keep ourselves imprisoned in. You will see how we shield part of our potential with the Curtain of the Painstake. Out of fear of being rejected by others we hide. In doing so we cover a part of the light that we could shine in this world.

As you read the examples in this chapter, you will come to see that this cover is a smokescreen: it is made up of assumptions, suspicions and speculations. Away with those, I say. Keeping ourselves, even partially, undercover does injustice not only to ourselves but to the whole. The world is not complete without your full participation in it. Your light is needed as much as that of the next person.

Once you see how you have pulled the curtain close and keep hidden, you can open it by adopting this practice:

1. **Train your ear** for the seemingly innocent sentences that allow you to stay within your comfort zone

2. **Tread** the if-then stairs and find the painstake by asking yourself how you would fill in the space of the dots that bode ill: "If I were to do that, then …"

3. **Trust** who you are now, the light that wants to shine

In the life stories below you will see how these three steps bring people back in touch with their potential, their inevitable ownness and 'silliness', their creativity, with the light that they have always been and forever will be.

First you will meet Elma, a woman who had the habit of thinking constantly about what she wanted to do without ever really coming into action. In our first contact she already touched on the life force that she had not felt for a long time. She came in heavy-hearted and left lightfooted, which marked the start of a trajectory of lightening up for her. I use the session with her as the basis for the theory of the painstake that keeps us trapped often without us being aware of it. Then I give seven other examples of people who were stuck, one of them being myself. The remedy I offer is simple. I just ask them to finish a particular sentence that we all use more often than we think: "If I were to do that, then …"

You will see the surprise that lies in store for those who finish their "If I were to do that, then …" sentences. Once the insight is gained, the shift is immediate. We reunite with a vital piece of ourselves long lost behind the Curtain of the Painstake. The examples also show how the theory evolved in real-time as I made these discoveries with the people in my private practice at the time. The theory comes forth from life. At the end of the chapter I summarize the three steps you can take for your own liberation into a lightfooted life.

Elma's Entry

Elma heard a radio interview with me. Astute, she found my number and once on the phone she got to the point straight away.

"I think you can help me climb out of the hole I find myself in. I just have to see you."

I had come to a point in my work that I did not take on new coaching clients, yet I made an appointment with her. I just couldn't shut the door on someone who approached me so directly.

On the day of our first meeting she seems a little shy. "I never do something like this," she says apologetically. "This is the first time I barge in on someone like this. I really am very happy that I can see you. I could jump with joy." She positively shines as she speaks.

We are still standing at the door but I am not letting this beautiful opening go by unnoticed. If Elma comes to me seeking to be happy and more who she is, I will make good use of the opportunity she unwittingly provides.

"If you could jump with joy, what's stopping you?"

"Well," she says with a laugh and a wave of her hand, "that was just a manner of speaking. I couldn't just jump and jive here with you, could I? If I were to do that ..."

She laughs and gives me a look of understanding. I know the ropes so I pretend that I don't get it. Inside I rejoice: we have only just met and we are right there at the Curtain of the Painstake. It couldn't be better.

When I don't make a move, Elma raises her eyebrow. She probably expected us to sit down and take time for her to tell her story and what is up in her life. This might take so long that we would only get to an intervention on my part next time – if there were to be a next time. But when you have come to talk with the intention of making a step, then you can't sit and do the usual thing. Then by definition you look for what is unusual; for what as humans we tend to push away out of fear that it is strange and unwanted; out of fear that we ourselves are somehow strange and unwanted. With all that this brings on. This is exactly what I am looking for with Elma. This is why I consciously keep us standing by the front door. Once we sit, it is much harder to get moving again. In a neutral tone of voice I ask:

"If you were to jump with joy here, then ..."

I look at her expectantly.

"Do you want me to finish this sentence?" She asks. She frowns, presses her lips together and then sighs. She looks longingly over my shoulder towards the sitting room.

"If you were to jump with joy here, then ...," I repeat.

"If I were to jump with joy here, then ... Well, you just can't do that with someone you've only just met!"

"If you were to jump with joy here, then ...," I repeat once more.

"If I were to jump with joy here, then ... then you and other people would find me weird," she says with a tone that conveys something like 'OK, have it your way; I hope you're done with your silly questions now'.

"If I and other people would find you weird, then ...?"

"If you and other people would find me weird, then soon no one would want to be around me." She sounds a bit angry now.

"If no one wants to be around you anymore, then ... "

"If no one wants to be around me anymore, then I will be alone."

"If you are alone, then ...,"

"If I am alone, I will die from loneliness."

I give her a moment to integrate where we have come to. We have done nothing more than turn her answers into next questions and in just a few steps we have landed at death.

"Of course you are not going to jump with joy here if you are afraid this will lead to your death," I say. "That is only fair. A child will understand that you do not consciously engage in an activity that you might die from."

She looks relieved and a little surprised at the same time. "I had no idea we would dip right into my fear," she says. "You waste no time, do you? From the time I was small, I have adapted to what I thought my parents wanted me to do. If you would have asked me what I came here for, I might not have given you a coherent answer. That is part of what I'm struggling with. I don't really know who I am anymore, because I always adapt to what I think others want me to be."

We all adapt when we are small. And that is not just a bad thing. It is the way we learn to be a human being within the family and the culture in which we are born. But as a small child we, of course, lack oversight. We cannot discern very well between situations in which we *really* need to adapt and those in which we *think* we need to adapt. Also we cannot distinguish between situations in which our parents want us to adapt momentarily or for ever and ever. As an adult we can read those situations far better, if we put our mind to it. Very often, though, we are so conditioned that we don't question what we think is right and proper.

I notice that Elma's right hand is on her heart and reassure her once more: "Of course you are not going to do something that you fear has the consequence of social death. Of course you're not going to risk your life here – you would be crazy to do so and I would not be right to suggest that. But as the adult that you are, you can ask yourself: is it true? Would it be likely that you would die of loneliness if you would jump with joy right here right now; if you would show more of your innate spontaneity? Or are we dealing with the fantasy of a child who is in every way still dependent upon her parents and other adult caregivers, because she cannot yet take care of herself?"

Elma nods with slow movements of her head. She looks down as if she needs a little time to take in what I am saying. When she looks up again, I continue.

"As a child you have to make sure that the people who take care of you stay with you. Instinctively you know that you will not make it on your own. Depending upon the situation in your family of origin, you have started to adapt and show acceptable behavior. Maybe your conclusion was that you shouldn't attract too much attention to yourself. Or that you shouldn't be a handful because your parents had enough to deal with already. But you are not a child anymore. You can take care of yourself very well. Do you think – as the adult that you are now – that you would die if you would jump with joy because of your daring step to come here?"

"Well, no, I will probably survive," Elma says with a tiny smile. She is visibly relieved when I finally walk away from the door. When she comes into the room behind me, I have already chosen a song to play. Bobby McFerrin blasts through the room with his *Don't worry be happy* and I start to dance. When Elma drops her bag on the floor and joins me, she turns out to be an incredible mover.

Why on earth shouldn't we dance with joy at any given moment of the day? Or behave in a way that differs from the usual? Our heart beats all of our lives. The sun always shines even when the sky is cloudy. Thousands have their birthday every day of the week all over the globe. There is always something to celebrate. So:

Music!

Dance!

Live!

Enjoy!

Step out of the painstake.

Death will not come to pass.

It will make you come alive.

The If-then Stairs

With Elma I went straight for the jugular. She had only just come in the door and already we started discovering the painstake. I have a trained ear for the seemingly innocent sentences "If I were to do that, then …". As you have seen I did no more than invite Elma to finish her thought. "If I were to jump with joy here, then …" In doing so this did not prove to be an innocent sentence at all. By keeping the question going through the use of the answers she gave, we landed at fear of death. Arriving at this fear of death in just a few steps is not only the case with Elma. When you or I make use of such a "If I were to do that, then …" statement, this is often because unconsciously we are afraid that through an unwanted action we will come to stand alone and die. That is what I call the painstake. The way of unmasking the painstake, I call the if-then stairs.

You have seen how the if-then steps worked with Elma. I only needed to ask what would happen if she would jump with joy. With the answer she gave: "Then you and other people would find me weird," I made the next question: "If I and other people would find you weird, then …?" And so we continued, from the one answer to the next question downward to a sure death.

Taking the if-then stairs often leads to fear of dying. We are scared to death to do things that we are not sure will be acceptable to others. No wonder that we don't feel fully free and happy. With this unconscious fear of death we shield part of our spontaneity, our potential, our life force. With the Curtain of the Painstake we hide part of the light that we are. The if-then stairs can also go up. In that case we do not end up at death but we gain new insight, new information on what you can do to respond to situations in a lightfooted way.

You will see how it works in the examples that I give from people who have become more lightfooted. Just like Elma they let themselves be hampered in their vitality and life force by assumptions they had never questioned before. Without being aware of it, they were stuck in the painstake. Developing an ear for sentences that allow you to stay in your comfort zone, unmasking the painstake by going down the if-then stairs and daring to see who you truly are – these three steps have helped them to unlock their natural spontaneity and originality. They take decisions more easily. They handle situations that knocked them out before in a lightfooted way now. They give themselves more freedom for courses of action that might not be usual but are effective. They allow themselves time to just be. They enjoy the moment.

Lightfooted in your Relationship

"If he doesn't want to move in with me now, then ..."

Vita can talk about her boyfriend who just doesn't want to take the step to living together for hours, and then some. She discusses her boyfriend and his reluctance to make a commitment to their relationship with her friends, her mother, her colleagues at work, well, with everyone she meets. Over time this has become a Big Issue.

Vita is having a hard time dealing with it. In her own eyes fate has not dealt her an easy hand. No telephone conversation, no dinner with friends or the Big Heavy All-encompassing Issue of the reluctant boyfriend is brought up. After years of well meant advice her friends don't know what to say anymore – even if they fully agree with her that he is a severe case of fear of committing, that after all these years he still doesn't want to grow up, that he just seems unable to show his true feelings for her ... that, to cut a long story short, it is all his fault. Her mother has grown a dislike for the man who causes her daughter anguish and pain. Colleagues sigh when Vita starts her litany again and dive behind their computers.

All this talking and laying awake at night has not brought Vita any further. She just keeps singing the same tune. What is behind her need to want to move in with this man who – despite her giving him a hard time about his reluctance – still adores her? We find out when she takes the if-then stairs:

"If he doesn't want to move in with me now, then maybe he never will."

"If maybe he never will, then I feel worthless."

"If I feel worthless, then I am worth nothing to anyone."

"If I am worth noting to anyone, I am better off dead."

So that is the thing. Vita has made her sense of self-worth fully dependent on living with her boyfriend. If he doesn't want to move in with her, she obviously is not worth the light of day and is better off dead. Vita has to recuperate for a moment now she sees that she puts a heavy load on the shoulders of this man whom she loves so much.

"What a bitch I am," she then says from the bottom of her heart.

It is not she who is a bitch. The real bitch is the very human capacity for self-reproach, that raises its angry head at any given opportunity. If you allow it to run its course, you jump out of the frying pan into the fire. Awareness is needed to remain out of its clutches. Self-reproach adds no value to life. It just brings you down. Better chase it away as soon as you are on to it.

Keep it Light

Do you know someone like Vita who easily falls into self-reproach and do you want to help her? Then do not follow up on her harsh self-judgment and keep it light. Before you know it, you are lost in long stories of how bad she is and has always been and how that might be the reason that her boyfriend … etcetera. Such conversations can go on forever without going anywhere. The only way forward is to stick to the essence of the conversation, for instance by making a general statement in a neutral tone of voice.

"Yes, we all have painstakes."

"Painstakes? What do you mean? I don't suffer from those. I am just an evil person. That must be the reason that he doesn't want to move in."

"Of course," I say with a smile, "if you are a bitch, then you will never have a man. If you have no man, then you have failed as a woman. If you have failed as a woman, then you might just as well call it a day. And if you call it a day, then it is game over, finito, death. I know the reasoning. It is a somewhat crooked way of our psyche to remain ahead of an ominous future. When we paint ourselves a doom scenario, reality might not be so bad. And if it is bad after all, then at least we came prepared. That is the idea. But this strategy doesn't really seem to work, does it? You for one don't seem to get very happy following this train of thought. So alight. Step out of this mode of thinking and let's take another look. Do you really think you are better off dead if he doesn't want to move in?"

Vita doesn't capitulate right away. "Then I will die of a broken heart."

I wait a moment and she starts again: "No. I would like nothing more than make a home together, but if in the end he doesn't want that, I will probably still breathe. Even if it is no fun at all without him."

"And have you seen what kind of information you have given yourself by taking the if-then stairs?"

She isn't sure what I mean. "Can you see that you have made your sense of self-worth fully dependent upon your boyfriend? That does not make you a bitch. But he obviously loves his freedom. Can you accept that? Can you take him as he is? Can you stop thinking that he ought to be different? Because if you make your sense of self-worth fully dependent upon him, you put him in a difficult position."

Vita is flabbergasted. "Wait a minute," she says. "If he doesn't want to move in with me now, then maybe he never will. If maybe he never will, then I feel worthless. If I feel worthless, then I am worth nothing to anyone. If I am worth noting to anyone, I am better off dead." So ... if I understand this well you say – or rather I say – that I equate his refusal to live with me to a death sentence. Aha! And you also say that in doing so I imply he is responsible for my life and my happiness. Yes, that is quite something. I fully understand that he does not want to take that on." Suddenly she starts to laugh. "That would frighten even me!"

Then thinking aloud she wonders if he might have a very good sense that she needs to be able to stand on her own two feet before he can take a next step with her. This insight leads to a whole new conversation between the two of them.

Lightfooted Dealing with a Dilemma

Rob, a young man who has lived in the Netherlands for a few years, considers moving back to his country of origin. He has had a great time here, in part because he quickly made a number of friends who helped him find his way. For weeks now he has been struggling with the decision to leave this good life behind and pick the thread of his life up again in the place he came from. Every time he has set a departure date, he comes back to it a few days later. He seems unable to make a clear-cut decision. He recognizes that he suffers from what his circle of friends call *mm: fear of missing out*. Yet he cannot escape from it. He keeps fretting. He wants to be in two spots at the same time and postpones deciding day by day. What keeps him from taking a decision?

"Yeah, what keeps me from making a choice. What keeps me here? The climate, of course, and the people. My friends have helped me immensely. I am so grateful to them and if I leave here, then …" He lets the words float into thin air. I, of course, invite him to finish his sentence.

He has to find words: "If I leave here ... if I leave here, I am an ungrateful bastard! I came here with nothing. I was no one. Now I have a company with amazing people who are really kind. We never fight, we have a good time at the office. It is inspiring to find people who share a vision. We think alike about our profession and the way of running a company. We have great plans for expansion and ..."

Again he goes down the well-trodden path of the story that he has told himself and others over and over again.

Don't get sidetracked

When someone uses a "If I were to do that, then …" sentence, more often than not there is an unconscious fear of death behind it. So you cannot blame the person for trying to find all kinds of escape routes and sideways to avoid coming to the point. This means you often are being offered long stories full of plausible reasons and explanations why a decision cannot possibly be taken or a choice is impossible to make at this time. On the one hand this and on the other hand that. Yes, how do you find your way out of a dilemma? As a friend, a partner, parent or coach you can be of assistance by sticking to the essence. This you do by calling them back to the if-then stairs in a friendly but insistent manner.

"If I am an ungrateful bastard, then ..." I repeat with a questioning look.

Rob shakes his head. It takes some time before he can find the words to express what he feels. His face betrays how painful it is for him to realize what he has just said. An ungrateful bastard is the last thing he wants to be. In an effort to escape the inevitable he again starts to speak highly of his friends here, how they have helped him in this culture that is so different from his own, how much he has learned … but this is not the issue. The issue is to get him to finish the next step on the if-then stairs that will give him insight in the painstake – and thus in the reason why he has not succeeded in taking a decision up until now.

Rob is not the only one to stall and try to find ways out of the predicament he is in. This is what we tend to do as human beings. We do all we can to move away from a spot of pain, to escape from what we find hard to stomach. In such cases we start to talk, and talk some more, all the time repeating what we already know. And so we waffle ourselves away from the issue at hand and immerse ourselves into our story over and over again.

This is the moment to call upon Rob to focus and to do this with a light touch. "I know you've had a good time here. This is a wonderful country and we are lovely people, but this is not the point now. We are now taking a look at whether it is on your life path to stay here or to go back home. If you really want to know the answer to that question, you should in my humble opinion finish the sentence. You said: 'If I leave here, I am an ungrateful bastard.' And if you are an ungrateful bastard, then …"

Rob needs to collect his thoughts. His head and heart have raced back again to the story of his good time here but after a short while he finally concedes:

"If I am an ungrateful bastard, then I lose my self-respect."

"If you lose your self-respect, then …"

He gets it now.

"If I lose my self-respect, then I can just as well put an end to it."

Once you have become familiar with the if-then stairs, then you know where you will end up – you end up at the pains-take that consists of the fear of dying. But how you get there is always a surprise. For Rob as well who had no idea that his doubtful going back and forth had to do with a sense of lack of gratitude and loss of self-respect.

He is startled. "Are you sure?" He asks. "Do you honestly think that I unconsciously sentence myself to death – that this is why I cannot settle the matter?"

He said it. I did not make it up. But what does he think: will leaving here truly lead to his death? Instantly, Rob realizes that the people he has befriended may have realized that he would not stay and live here forever. When he decides that his time here is up, this by no means signifies that he is not grateful to his friends and colleagues. He realizes that he would not begrudge anyone the right to follow his or her own path. Even if that means that you disappear from each other's daily life. On the spot he decides to give a good farewell party for the people he has grown to love.

Remaining Lightfooted When Set Back

I am starting to see a pattern. Invariably it seems that walk-ing down the if-then stairs, leads to death and so we don't. We stay put and do not venture out into the area that we mark with the …. We let our "If I were to do that, then …" sentenc-es hang in midair and nod to each other our silent agreement on this no-go area. Until you go there. Facing a fear turns out not to be half as bad as not facing it. Remember those years when you – or maybe it was your little sibling – had a fear of something bad under the bed? How could you sleep with that thing there? I admired my mother who was not afraid to have a look while I was shivering under the covers. When she made me go on my knees and inspect the space under my bed, I argued the frightening thing could appear any minute out of thin air. So she crept under my bed and invited me to lay there with her for a while. I fell asleep in her arms. The next evening I took a quick look but soon I forgot what had been so frightening to me before. Many of us have similar stories that we relegate to our young years. But some child-time fears are still alive in us and remain so, until we shed light on them. And just when I think I have my theory down pat, the if-then stairs take another turn.

Meet Nesra. My first impression of her is that she is a fighter. She tells me she has received a bad review at work and she doesn't know how to deal with it. Can I help? We shall see. What is required is that she gives up her attitude that none of this has anything to do with her. She nor I can change her colleagues. We can only have a look at her part in this situation. "What do you mean? They have nothing on me. I do what's expected. And more. They should take me as I am, or …," she says belligerently.

Nesra's 'or', followed by an ominous silence, seems a variation on the now familiar 'if-then…'

"If they don't take you as you are, then…?"

"Then… What!" Nesra is not in the mood for a game. Her eyes spit fire. She is angry. She wants someone to be fully on her side and walk the street of indignation to the end. I know this is a cul-de-sac, but OK. If this is the way she can cool down a bit, I am happy to accommodate her.

"I understand how you feel. Of course, it is no fun to receive a bad review, especially when you yourself feel this is completely unjust. No wonder you are outraged. I get that. And we can see how you can move on with this. What happens if they don't take you as you are? Then …?"

"If they don't take me as I am, then that is their loss!" She snaps.

"And if it is their loss, then …"

"If it is their loss, then maybe they will finally start to notice what happens if I no longer fulfill that post. They have no idea of all the work I do. They just don't see it."

In impotent rage Nesra hits the side of the chair with her hand. "They just don't see what I contribute by taking on all kinds of tasks that remain undone!" This time taking the if-then stairs has not led us downward as I have gotten used to. Nesra's faith in her own capacities and her way of seeing what she contributes seem to steer the stairs in the other direction. Upwards. I give her a next step:

"If they don't see what you do and how much you contribute, then …"

"If they don't see what I do and how much I contribute, then … then maybe I should show them?!"

She ends the sentence with a question mark and her face looks like one as well. This clearly is something she has not considered yet. She has always assumed that you just have to do your job in a quiet and responsible manner. She hates people who constantly brag about themselves. Bloated frogs is what she calls them. And she will die before becoming one of them.

The way this conversation with Nesra develops is a surprise for me, too. Up until now when taking the if-then stairs, they would invariably lead to death. This is the first time that someone actually comes to a possible solution of the matter at hand. So after Nesra has left, I retrace our steps. How was Nesra's approach different from those of the others with whom I have been doing this exercise, I find myself wondering. Nesra started out with indignation. She was convinced of her own way of seeing things, of being right and of her own value. That is exactly the difference. In other conversations people were stuck in endless thought loops. They held themselves back or doubted their own self-worth. Not Nesra. Not for a moment did she consider the point of view of her boss to be right. Her positive outlook on herself made the if-then stairs go up instead of downwards. So here is a whole new application!

When we next met, Nesra said she had consulted with a trusted colleague. This person confirmed that she had no idea of the amount of work that Nesra gets done. Simply because she hardly speaks of what she does. The feedback was that she is apt to be interested in the work of others but keeps silent when it is her turn to share. That is useful information. Nesra has taken it on board and has started to experiment with ways to show colleagues and bosses what she does in a day.

"It doesn't come easy," she says. "I don't really know how to tell people what I do without it sounding like I boast. I am afraid that people will find me a show-off if I talk too much about what I do."

We apply the if-then stairs:

"If I talk too much about what I do, then people will think I am a show-off."

"If people think I am a show-off, then they might not like me."

"If they don't like me, they will avoid me."

"If they avoid me, I will be left to my own devices."

"If I am left to my own devices, I will die."

Apparently Nesra is scared to death to be held for a boaster. She is well aware where that comes from, she says. And she tells the story of a girl in school who was given the cold shoulder by others because of her beautiful clothes. That experience made Nesra decide that she would never ever pride herself on anything.

"She couldn't help it that her parents had more to spend than we did," she says now. "But we wanted to have nothing to do with her. She was never allowed in on our games. Quite harsh now that I come to think of it."

While she tells this story from her youth, I think hard. Why did we have the stairs lead upward last time and now we are back on the downward slope? In a flash, I see why: the first sentence of the if-then stairs determines the outcome. Last time Nesra was convinced that she was right. Now her first sentence is full of self-reproach. It holds a negative judgment.

Judgment alert

When the first if-then sentence contains a negative judgment, the stairs will inevitably lead to death. The negativity can be held in a word, for instance in Nesra's 'too much' in the first sentence: "If I talk too much about what I do, then ..." It can also be the tone in which the sentence is spoken, such as in the basic example: "If I were to do that, then ..."

Once you are aware of this, you can start to play with the direction the stairs are taking. You can do the exercise with a negative judgment in the first sentence and see where you get to. Then you can turn the first sentence into a positive and see what information that produces.

Nesra has a questioning look on her face. She has noticed that I was not paying full attention to her story of the past. "Are you not interested in the source of my fear?" She asks.

"You're a good observer," I say. "I confess to being more interested in your future than in your past. I was wondering where the if-then stairs lead to when you start with a neutrally formulated first sentence."

Briefly I explain to Nesra what I am starting to find. That you end up at death when your initial sentence comprises a doubt or negative judgment, and that you are given new insight when you start out with a positive first sentence. I don't yet know what happens when you start with a neutral sentence, a statement that describes a situation without any trace of judgment or direction.

Nesra is beginning to enjoy our exchange. Together we try to come up with a neutral initial phrase. We soon come to: "If I talk about what I do, others know what keeps me occupied." That is an observation, a fact without a negative or positive charge. She knows how to proceed:

"If I talk about what I do, others know what keeps me occupied."

"If others know what keeps me occupied, we can coordinate our efforts."

"If we coordinate our efforts, this will work for all of us."

Nesra is surprised and happy at the same time.

"So it is possible to be just neutral," she says. "That is way less exhausting than when I am so indignant, because I feel that they don't see my contribution, or when I am scared to show off. It is as if I only now realize that I am a colleague of these people; that I am as much part of the whole enterprise as they are."

This is a big realization for this young woman who has always had the idea that she was somehow an outsider. For me, too, this neutral position is a discovery that I have wanted to make for a long time. Myself, I like being like an empty channel through which life can flow freely without being hooked by fear that originates in the past or anxiety about the future. In that neutral empty mode you do not react to what another says from a pattern once established, but you take what happens as information. You can remain attentive when someone puts something forward that is not in line with the way you view the world. There is no need to combat the other with words or make them bad in your own thoughts. You are being given a glimpse into the inner world of another person. That is all. Such an attitude saves you a lot of excitement and allows you to get to know the other better. Because it is only interesting when someone else sees issues differently from you.

The feelings that someone else's words or actions evoke in you are also information. Apparently you are sensitive in this area. That is interesting. What is behind this sensitivity? Taking the if-then stairs can help you surface information on this point. And again and again facing your fear of death. You will notice that this fear evaporates the more light you shine on it.

Nesra has the last word.

"And if it works for all of us, yahoo, then I get to stay, I will not lose my job and I might even one day be boss myself!"

She makes me laugh when she makes fun of the method, of me and of herself in this way. I would not be surprised if this young lady would make a fine career. I for one am grateful to her. Exploring together we have found a good addition to the if-then repertoire. The stairs go up or down depending upon the charge of the initial sentence. If you start with a judgment, you will end at death; if you begin with a positive approach, you'll get new insight. A neutral first sentence renders neutral and factual information. If Nesra is more open about her work, she makes it easier for others to cooperate with her and she gets the feeling that she belongs. Once she saw that, it silenced us both. The upward stairs make you happy, but also skirt over the surface a bit. The neutral position is not a stairway anymore – you stay horizontal in the now as it is. That is more like a passage. A passageway.

Lightfooted to the Next Phase of Life

Both the upward stairs and the passageway turn out to be a helpful addition to my repertoire. At a party of a friend I meet Paul. We have met before at the house of our mutual friend, so we strike up a conversation. The company he works for is reorganizing, he tells me, and people over 57.5 are given the opportunity to leave with a handsome deal. Paul tells me how much he loves his work. Not a hair on his head that considers leaving this organization that he joined at 23.

"No way. What on earth should I do if I don't get up and go to work every day?"

The door to the if-then stairs is wide open, but I am at a party and I do not want to be playing the coach here. Can I still engage with him in a way that is meaningful without me being the professional? As so often before, I learn that there is no need for me to take a decision. If I just keep my heart open, the conversation will flow and take its own course. This time it is Paul's partner who subtly reminds him that he often comes home tired and discontented, that he has been complaining for a while about not being able to keep up with the pace of change and that he has exactly the age that they target with the goodbye deal.

"It is my life. I will see where I go with this," Paul snaps. His partner wisely keeps silent. He has known his love for a while.

"I can't just stop working from one day to the next?" Says Paul with a sigh in my direction and a facial expression that is designed to make me believe that what he says is irrefutably true.

"Why is that so?" I ask, following my natural curiosity. His partner throws me a quick look. Paul's answer is immediate:

"If I stop working, that will be my death. Not only will I no longer be anyone in the world, I will also literally die. I will die of boredom."

Naked and unreserved, the whole painstake is laid out between us. Paul looks away. I ask a next question.

"Well, of course, you shouldn't do what leads to certain death. But do you really think you will be bored to death? Don't you have hobbies or interests?"

Paul shrugs. He takes a sip of wine. It is clear that he is not too happy with the direction this conversation is taking.

"What would you do if you had all the time in the world?" I try again.

"If I had all the time in the world, then ..."

"If I had all the time in the world, I wouldn't have a clue how to fill it!"

I look into my glass and keep silent. From the corner of my eye I see that Paul's partner gives me an almost imperceptible nod and then seemingly concentrates again on observing the other guests. His ears are clearly with our conversation. Paul reconsiders.

"OK, if I had all the time in the world, and the money, I would love to go and live in Italy for a while. Yes, I do think I could keep myself busy and entertained there for a few months."

"Italy – wonderful!" I respond. "And what would happen if you did move to Italy for a few months?"

"Well, I wouldn't be going by myself, of course. And so if we were to go to Italy for a few months, I would want to take an Italian language course beforehand. And also I would want to listen to the great operas before going to see them there."

As he gets up, Paul's partner gives me a secret thumbs up. There might still be a long way to go before Paul leaves the organization that has clearly been his life. But life after early retirement might not look as empty and grim as before. Someone embraces me from behind and gives me a smack on the cheek.

"Come on, Paul," I hear his partner say. "Dinnertime. Let's go get Italian!"

Mistrust truisms

The if-then sentences are not the only way in which we scrupulously try to avert conversations that unconsciously we suspect do not bode well. Often the if-then construction is preceded by other attempts to steer a conversation in another direction. We are all well trained in the use of statements that seem innocent but that upon closer inspection serve the same purpose: game over. If you are on the way to develop yourself, it is up to you to not let the game end here. It is up to you to practice opening the Curtain of the Painstake.

Truisms is the name for these customary sentences with which we try to divert someone in a conversation. When someone uses a truism, you often notice a strange ending to a conversation. There is something inconclusive about it that makes you feel uncomfortable. Usually we solve such an awkward situation by changing the subject. We swiftly move away from the truism to talk about something else. Everyone is relieved when that move works and the conversation can start again as if nothing has happened. But then all stays as it was. Nothing gets solved.

Truisms come in all sorts of variations. Sometimes a truism is like a subtly placed dam in a stream that almost imperceptibly changes its direction. At other times you will experience a truism like a steel door, a safe that has no easy access. In her Harry Potter-books J.K. Rowling uses the term Death Eaters for the obscure followers of the dark lord He-who-must-not-be-named. This is exactly what truisms are meant to do: eat the sentence that might lead to supposed death.

Examples of truisms or death eaters:

"So..."

"And you don't want that to happen."

"I can't just ..."

"Ah, well, this is how things go..."

"If you would know all beforehand ..."

"You cannot always have your way."

"There are no guarantees in life, are there?"

"I would like to, but ..."

"It's not at our bidding, is it?"

"That is just how the cards have been dealt ..."

"Not for me!"

"If this is the way it is, what can you do?"

"You can't do much if you're on your own..."

"I tried, but ..."

"We shall see how it turns out..."

"You've got to get lucky, or else ..."

"It's not up to us ..."

"Of course, you can't do that."

Notice the dots here, too. People who make use of a truism to change the subject of the conversation often look at you with a knowing glance. As if to say: you, of course, also understand that it is irrefutably and indisputably true what I say here and would you please leave it at that?

If you want to proceed and live a lightfooted life, then be on the alert. Practice listening and do not be led astray by trivial truisms. Ask a next question and you will find out that such a truism is often followed by a "If …, then …." And you by now know what you can do.

From Livid to Lightfooted

Then, one day, I find myself in a grumpy mood. I am getting crabby about minutes of a meeting that have not been sent. Our next meeting is coming up and as the leader of the pack I want the minutes ready in time. I have asked, I have pleaded, I have amended them myself and still I cannot get the secretary to distribute them. As I walk to my computer ready to type the menacing message I have been rehearsing under the shower, I catch myself. What am I doing getting so worked up? What is really happening here? Or rather: what am I thinking? When I stop to listen, I hear a familiar inner voice booming:

"If those minutes aren't being distributed in time, then …"

Aha! So that is what is bugging me. I investigate what I am afraid of, knowing full well where I will end up. But how I get there, is always interesting. So there I go:

"If those minutes aren't distributed in time, my colleagues may think I am sloppy."

"If my colleagues think I am sloppy, they will not value me highly."

"If they do not value me highly, they will not want me on the Board."

"If they don't want me on the Board, I will be rejected."

"If I am rejected, I will be an outcast."

"If I am an outcast, I will be alone and I will die."

So that is why I am being so pushy – or some would say, aggressive. A part of me thinks that my fate as a member of this board depends entirely on the timely delivery of these minutes. That's what is making me livid. I am aggressive out of fear. With this insight I can breathe again. Immediately my colleague the secretary turns from some sort of adversary to another human being who has lots of things happening in her life. And there is still time. That, too, had become obscure. It is still is a full two weeks until the day we meet. I relax and grab the phone. Now I can have a kind and constructive conversation. I can be in relationship with my own fears, with her priorities and with the work we are engaged in together. And we can make light together of the many things that need doing before anything gets done.

Lightfooted in Dealing with Mail

This story was told to me by a young woman who works hard and is good at her job. I have seen her at work and was impressed by her professionalism. She herself has a tendency to think that she doesn't do enough and is not good enough. Through our cooperation she is aware of the if-then stairs. And this is how she showed herself on a warm summer evening that there is a time for work and a time to relax.

"One Friday evening I sat outside with friends. Everyone had had a busy week and we were just having a good time, cracking jokes – you know how it is. Suddenly I wondered if I could really take the evening off. I had made my targets but I could, of course, have sent a couple of more emails. Some clients I had not been in touch with for some time. I made a remark to this effect and my friends nodded as if to say:

'Yeah, if you don't maintain your client network, then …'

It was exactly like you say. No one knows exactly what will happen, but everyone suspects that the story does not have a happy ending. The mood changed and I hadn't yet figured out what caused this. I started to work my phone when a friend of mine asked:

'Is it really that bad, Maria, that you have not sent those emails this week? You are good at what you do, aren't you? Do you think people forget you just like that? My perception is that everyone is always on the lookout for people who are capable and who meet their deadlines. Didn't you say you had met your targets? Your clients were happy, weren't they? So, please relax, girl. There are always more mails to be sent than a normal person can get to on a day. We all have to live with what we don't get done. Next week there is another week, now it is Friday night. Come on – enjoy!'

It doesn't happen to me often, but this time I was silenced. Because, yeah, what happens if I don't maintain my client network? The comments of my friend made me remember the if-then stairs. Inwardly, I took the stairs down:

"If I don't maintain my client network, then they will replace me with someone else."

"If they replace me with someone else, then I can ..."

And in a flash I saw that I could reason both ways. I saw how I put myself under stress when I finished the sentence this way:

"If they replace me with someone else, then very soon I cannot pay my rent."

That made me shiver. I cannot bear the thought that I would have to leave my wonderful sweet place. If I would continue down that train of thought, I would soon be out on the street and yes, I know where my ominous predictions lead: then I will end all by myself in the gutter.

But I saw clearly that there was another option, one more in the neutral direction that my friend pointed to. How many mails can a person send in one day?

"If they replace me with another, then they obviously don't recognize my value and fortunately myself I do."

The weather was nice and we stayed outside the whole evening. It had been a long time since I could relax the way I did that night."

On the other side of diffidence lies a lightfooted existence that people who are unaware of being trapped in the painstake can only dream of. It is not so that all your worries will be over forever once you learn to live the lightfooted life, but you will worry less. You quit the assembly line in the factory of worries. All the time you spent worrying will now be yours to do with as you please or see fit. With this time at your disposal you can see what is realistic in the moment. You can see yourself with new eyes. Eyes that are not colored by fear of what might happen or pain of what once was the case. You will gain more confidence in yourself and in life. You will begin to realize that all that you need is already inside you.

Lightfooted in Carrying Responsibility

Steven knows how to push himself. He has always been someone who has needed ample time to come to a decision; considered decisions, as he likes to say. In the new job that he covets wholeheartedly, it looks as if his slowness has grown. Sometimes he just can't figure out what to do, he admits over dinner one day. He relates how he spends more and more time behind his desk where he stares at proposals and figures until his eyes water. When he receives questions – "Has he determined the course of action for project X yet?" – His thoughts start to scramble. Ceaselessly the thoughts in his head call out to him: "Take a decision. Settle the matter. If you do not take a decision now, then …"

Now Steven does not have one problem, but two. Apart from having to come to a decision on a wise course of action, now he must also combat the damning judgment that he pronounces on himself. He confesses that he considers resigning from his post and start his own business. That seems a drastic step to me. And taking drastic steps is not like him. So I suggest that he finishes the sentence that he torments himself with: "If you don't take a decision now, then …"

In one go he lays out this painstake:

"If I don't take a decision now, then I am a loser."

Steven works at a level in which he needs to take crucial decisions. He hasn't climbed up the organizational ladder for no reason. He might not be the fastest on the team, but I have known him for years and he certainly is not a loser. Never has been. He needs time to come to a decision but without fail he comes with a sound proposal that is well thought through. His obvious stress moves me and I tell him of my concept of lightfooted living. Then I ask him to finish the sentence: "If I am a loser, then…"

"If I am a loser, then I might lose my job."

"If I lose my job, I might never find work again."

"If I never find work again, then I am lost forever."

"I never quite knew what I was afraid of, so this is very revealing," he comments. "No wonder I am stressed out when deep down I am convinced that I will be lost forever. It just happens to take some time for me to get clarity. If I don't take that time, then ..."

I need only look at him and there he goes again:

"If I don't take the time to get clarity, then I might take the wrong decision."

"If I take the wrong decision, that can impact many people negatively."

"If a bad decision on my part would impact many people negatively, then I would die of shame – ah, death, there we are again!"

Steven nods a few times and falls silent.

Don't say a word

Not saying anything is often the best strategy. More often than you like you have to keep quiet, look at the floor and sit on your hands. Do not become impatient and start to fill the gap. Let time go by and keep your heart open. Just wait until the other person is ready to start talking again.

After a while he says: "I feel more confident. My approach works. I have been appointed to this post for good reason. People who think everything needs to move faster have their qualities. But my quality is that I can see through complex issues and find the direction we are to go. I would die of shame if I made a mistake I could have avoided because I gave in to the pressure from the organization. And I am not ashamed at all to stand for my approach. Is that lightfooted living, too?"

Whatever it is, he looks much better than when we started this conversation.

"I get it," he says while he arches himself towards me over the table, "lightfooted living is an inner quality, a way of dealing with who you are as a unique being. It is not to cave in under the pressure of expectations that may or may not be held by others, but shine your own light."

In his suit he looks like a seasoned businessman, but now he talks like me. This makes me think we can take another step forward. I ask him how he deals with decisions around his family that, after his divorce and second marriage, has a complex composition. "If I need to take a decision on the home front, I go outside. I need only walk the dog for a few blocks and I know what to do."

Would he consider going outside for a walk next time he needs to ponder a difficult decision, I ask. The park is not too far from his office, I know.

"You know I can't do that," is his first response.

"Why not?"

"Well, if everyone went outdoors over every decision they need to take, then soon no one is left in the office. And if there is no one left in the office, we might as well close down."

The if-then stairs are laid out in all their splendor. And with a curious twist as Steven unwittingly no longer talks about himself. He has generalized the statement. He went from "I" to "everyone".

No good generalizations

If you don't pay attention, you won't notice that something personal all of a sudden goes for each and every one. This is another clever way that we unwittingly use to get out of something. "If I do this now, then soon everyone will." It is the kind of threat that again needs to make sure you don't need to alter your behavior and all can stay as it always was.

"This brings us right back to death," I say. "What I call the painstake. That makes you stay put behind your desk as you always do. Then nothing needs to change. You remain where you are until the cows come home. But isn't your company poised on innovation? By any definition innovation is doing what is unusual, not yet done before. Does that go only for the products you make and the services you deliver or can that spirit of innovation also be applied to the way you work?".

"Touché," Steven laughs: "I am aware of your motto: how you are is what you bring into the world. And you have a point. We don't really apply innovation to ourselves and the way we organize ourselves or our work."

I push on: "So if you do not generalize but apply this to yourself only. And if you do not assume that you will go outdoors for any old decision but only for the big ones – what do you say?"

"OK. So, if I go for a walk when I need to take a big decision, then …"

"If I go for a walk when I need to take a big decision, then I can get clear more easily."

"If I can get clear more easily, then I can come to a decision faster."

"If I can come to a decision faster, then the whole organization benefits."

Aha! If Steven does not apply the option to do something unusual to the fictive everyone but only to himself, he follows a completely different reasoning. Then a possibility opens for him to solve something that has been troubling him for years. This is not only of benefit to himself but to the whole organization.

"If I am a better decision-maker by going out for a bit, then I might inspire others to approach their work more creatively."

"If we start to work more creatively as an organization, then not only does the work become more enjoyable, we might also come up with more creative solutions for our clients."

"If we come up with more creative solutions for our clients, then as an organization we can grow from strength to strength."

Three Steps to Lightfooted Living

Everything that you want to be able to do well, you have to practice over and over again. Ask the prima ballerina who can only maintain her high level by training on a daily basis without fail. To be lightfooted the same holds true. These next three steps are helpful if you want to draw the Curtain of the Painstake open and establish yourself in lightfooted living day by day. Help yourself to lighter feet first. The dance with others will naturally become more elegant.

1. **Train your ear** for the seemingly innocent sentences that allow you to stay within your comfort zone

2. **Tread** the if-then stairs and find the painstake by asking yourself how you would fill in the space of the dots that bode ill: "If I were to do that , then …"

3. **Trust** who you are now, the light that wants to shine brightly

1. Train your ear

Listen to what you say. Note when you use a truism or hide behind an if-then phrase. In the moment make a conscious choice. Be honest about whether this is a good moment to show yourself fully to the one you are with by continuing the conversation. Do you feel safe enough? Is the other person a true friend or a person with compassion? If so, gather your courage and walk the if-then stairs. If not, then tie a knot in your hankie and make sure that you take a closer look at yourself later. For some people it works best to do this exercise on a fixed time of day: on the way home after work or just before going to bed. Look back on your day, identify a truism you used and walk the if-then stairs.

Scientists tell us that it takes 21 days to form a new habit. That is exactly what you are doing by revealing your painstakes and learning to be lighter on your feet. You might want to record your truisms each day so you can read them back and discover in what situations you take refuge in backing off. Don't only jot down what you say but also consider your inner dialogue, the conversation that you conduct with yourself. Also take into account what you did not say on any given day as a consequence of thinking "If I were to say that, then …". Recording what you say and think will give you an impression of the progress you are making. This progress will be palpable in a reduced fear of rejection. You will notably worry less about what others think. You will more easily give free reign to your innate curiosity. This will help in making easy contact with strangers and digging deeper with those you know. You will notice that you react less and act more often. You do as you see fit; from the heart, as the light that you are.

2. Tread the stairs and discover the trap

Did you catch yourself on a truism or another statement that likewise ends with the ominous dot, dot, dot? Do the if-then stairs, finish the sentence that otherwise you would let hang in the air. Ask yourself out loud or in silence:

> "If I give in to that, then …"

or: "If I start to do that, then …"

or: "If I can't even manage this, then ...?"

And then you proceed:

- "If I ....

    then..."

- "If I ....

    then..."

- "If I ....

    then..."

- "If I ....

    then..."

- "If I ....

  then..."

- "If I ....

  then..."

When you end up at the painstake – the fear that no single soul on earth will want to be around you anymore – you do the *reality check*. How probable is this? Often you will see that in truth this fear stems from your childhood. As a child we have been afraid at times that we would not make it. Maybe your mother did not come right away when you woke up hungry as a newborn. Your little baby body was wrecked with agony, since how could you be sure that someone would ever show up to feed you and keep you from starvation right there and then? As a toddler you might have been naughty and sent to bed without being given dinner. From these and other such instances a fear sprung up that somehow you would not belong anymore.

Maybe you got lost in the supermarket or during a walk on the beach or in the zoo. These are all moments in which the adrenalin sweeps through the body: if you were to stay behind alone as a child, then there is a fair chance of an unhappy ending. This will not happen very easily in reality, but it does happen easily in our lively childhood imagination.

When by walking down the if-then stairs, you arrive at death, then it is helpful to allow yourself to feel the fear consciously as the adult you are now. Fear that is being felt resolves itself and ebbs away. Repeating this each time you go down the if-then stairs, you will slowly and surely lighten up. This brings you closer and closer, or rather opener and opener to lightfootedness: the inner attitude that will allow you always to see more ways than one to bake a cake, to overcome an obstacle, to be with what is.

Of course, you can also practice with positively charged sentences like:

- "If I make my dreams come true, then...................... ...."

- "If I become more myself, then................................. ...."

- "If I am in my element, then...................................... ...."

Can you feel what happens to you when you work with these positively charged statements? Do you feel your heart sing? Do your shoulders relax while you weren't even aware of being tense there before? Do you feel considerably lighter? If so, then there is no reason to begrudge yourself this treat on a regular basis. You can think whichever way suits you. You are the boss of what happens inside your head. So you can opt for thoughts that lift you up and promote lightfootedness. Treat yourself consciously on a daily portion of lightfootedness and notice how differently you approach life and all the situations it presents you with. You'll be light on your feet, curious what each day will bring.

- "If I meet people with an open heart, then...............
....
...."

- "If I can listen deeply to myself and others, then....
....
...."

- "If I can accept people as they are, then...................
....
...."

3. Trust who you are now, the light that wants to shine brightly

You are not your thoughts or the patterns in which you tend to think. You are the consciousness that observes these patterns and thoughts. You are the light. In the cinema the projector brings a movie to life with all its fictional characters. For an hour and a half you watch with fascination what these people live through. You share their life, their ups and down and their emotions. If the lamp of the projector is turned off, the images stop. The screen is the white screen on which anything can be projected. An action movie or a romantic comedy – the white screen never changes. Nor does the lamp in the projection room. It stays the same whatever is on the reel. The same holds true for the light that we are, the light of consciousness that shows us the movie of our lives. Whatever happens, the light remains unchanged. That is who you are in essence.

When you remember who you are and keep realizing this, it will be easier for you to step out of patterns of thinking that are based on a speculation about the future or an interpretation of your past. You can alight the train of thoughts and know yourself as a light, part of all light. You will dance with life with all its chances and challenges on a lighter footing. Surrender and you will experience that there was never anything to gain, only to experience. To experience exactly the way it is. Painful, delightful – life doesn't mind. You happen. You are an amazing, dazzling, alightful happening of life.

Lifelight

Born you are not just once
On the day we call your birthday
From then on
The day that you first saw the light
And that we celebrate each year
Happy you are here
Happy you are who you are
Happy about who you are still to become

Born you are each time you realize
How improbably unique it is
That you are who you are
With all your qualities and gifts
With your intuitions and your outbursts
With your ins and your outs
That make you you

Born you are each time
When you not only
See the light outside
But also experience the light within
Your inner light
Your lifelight
The light that you can shine
The light with which you can create
The light in you which is one with the all

All one
Is different from alone
You cannot think yourself alone
When you know yourself all one

LIGHTHEADED

light•head•ed (līt′hĕd′ĭd) adj.

1. Faint, giddy, or delirious: lightheaded with wine.

2. Given to frivolity; silly.

Proposal to thefreedictionary.com:

3. Apt in letting the inner light shine without any filtering from the past or the future.

Lightheaded living is being able to see without filters clouding your perception. It is being aware at each moment of what happens inside and around you without making interpretations and stories. It is looking at the world ever afresh, free from judgments that stem from what you have had happen before. Free from expectations of a possible future. It is living as if you have only this very moment available to you. And this one. And this. Every second of existence is fully new. Never occurred before and over before you know it. No need to grieve as life keeps giving new moments all the time.

Lightheaded people live an intense life and at the same time remain exceptionally calm. They are able to observe their thoughts and emotions without going along with them. They always remain in the same place. They do not let themselves be swept off their feet by indignation or anger, by enthusiasm or desire. They see the emotions, and are not them. They have thoughts, and don't necessarily act accordingly. They have practiced not to identify with the ever-changing landscape of emotions and thoughts. The source of their action is and remains the light. They remain one with the light.

This makes lightheadedness not something you learn one day and then have mastered forever and ever. It is a practice for life. Just like the top tennis player who keeps practicing his serve and the star pianist who plays the scales daily to stay in shape, lightheaded life requires regular practice. Time and again the one who practices lightheadedness wants to remember the inner light. Also in situations that are challenging. Also in times that are hard. Then especially the art is to continue to see yourself as light. And from this realization see the light in the other.

The Curtain of the Many Stories

Stories are more dangerous than many people think. Something happens. Someone says or does something and you react. Later you rewind the tape of this occurrence and you give meaning to what took place. In this way a story is born that helps you make meaning, from your vantage point, of what happened. You tell your story to someone who is interested and this person gives his or her response. You integrate this. Next time you tell the story, it has slightly changed. You have behaved just a bit better than really was the case. The other is just a bit stranger or more stupid, acted slightly more awkward or unkind. Slowly but surely this makes for a distorted view.

Even a well-trained volleyball player hits the ball in the net during a crucial game sometimes. In the same way it happens that people who practice lightheadedness lose it. Then they leave the light state in which they dwell and see another as other, as a threat for their inner peace or their way of living. They express themselves with harsh words or a look of irritation. Until they remember that they are a light. That there is no need ever to leave the place of light – that in actual fact you cannot leave it. You can only feel left out when for a moment you forget who you truly are. Like when you have lost yourself in a story, a story of justified anger, sorry victimhood or assumed arrogance.

A story is made in an instant. In no time at all it takes you with it and makes you believe that you are right, that you are better or to the contrary, worse, that you should stand up for yourself. Until we realize what it is we are doing. Until we become conscious that with our stories we make a lame attempt to put ourselves in a favorable light; on the basis of our past; on the basis of what happened once, long ago or just recently. But what is here now? What can happen right here right now when we do not go into defense but are open and listen to what another has to say? Isn't that many times more interesting than going down memory lane and discussing yesterday's news?

In this chapter I tell a parable about a land where the people polished their stories until they shone. So that they were a beautiful perfect reflection of what they had all been through. The people in this land were at it day and night. They spent so much time on the perfection of their stories that they forgot who they were. Because people are not their stories. They are not even the main characters in their stories.

The parable below shows how you can withdraw your attention from the stories that without exception deal with what you experienced in the past or expect from the future, that is, how you can cut yourself loose from the ever-changing thoughts about yourself and your circumstances. At the end of the chapter I shed light on three exercises that you can use to stay out of the grip of stories. You shall see you can lighten your view of the world, and thus at the world around you.

The Land of Stained Glass

Sometime, not far away or long ago, some human being was busy day and night making the most beautiful stained glass window the world had ever laid eyes on. Everything that happened to this human was processed in color and form in the big narrative in stained glass. The transparent yellow pieces related of youthful summers full of carefree sandcastle building on the beach, running after butterflies and playing with other children until sundown. Deeper ochre marked the many moments of bliss in which this human had felt seen and known deeply, had a sense of being part of the immeasurable expanse of the cosmos. Times of grief were visible as dark spots that, dim and obscure, told tales of losses incurred. The acute absence of loved ones were given a spot in this way as well as the inner pain that plagued the soul from time to time. Despair of days that the distance to the world seemed unbridgeable and anger about the imperfection of life on earth were represented in dark greyblack planes. The frequent fiery red related of adventures in the realm of love, hearts won and broken, the connection with one other human that was made and how this deepened and deepened over the years. Friendships from long ago as well as current ones, growth in work and how this person saw themselves and felt – in short: all that this human experienced in life was reproduced in a variety of form and color in the stained glass window.

For hours this human could ponder where to put a certain occurrence. And this human was not the only one who processed what happened in life in this manner. Family, neighbors and friends did exactly the same. Days and days they could speak in depth of the way the window had gotten its specific shape. Each in their own way worked on the perfect representation of their lives in their own stained glass windows.

When they got together, they shared what had happened to them in recent times and how they had represented this in the window of their lives. They listened, sympathized and gave each other good council. They educated their children in the art of the multifaceted representation of life lived. And so a whole culture of stained glass window people came into being.

One day a stranger came to town with friendly eyes and an interested look on his gentle face. Passionately the people enlightened this attentively listening stranger about their stained glass windows. Diligently they explained the structure in their window, the choices of color they had made, each one an expert in their own experience and translation into the form their window had taken on. The stranger listened attentively, asked questions that were a mark of his sincere interest and indicated patterns that seemed similar in several windows he had seen. That last comment was not appreciated by each and all. The people all preferred to have their own window be unique. Patterns in their own portrayal were one thing, but that these bore a resemblance to those in others, that their very own rendition of experiences and thoughts would be predictable - that they would rather not hear.

They began to notice that the stranger never passed judgment on the complexity of a window or gave a compliment about the beauty of composition and execution. Out of a sense of curiosity, one day they invited the stranger to a conversation.

At the agreed time the people congregated. The question was asked and the stranger answered:

"You devote all the time you have to perfecting the stained glass windows that are superb and exquisite, each and every one of them. Each of you is a master in the craft of making these windows. Your supremacy is unquestioned, your choice of color outstanding. Your representation will not fail to move anyone who lays an eye on them. It is undisputed that you all are well versed in how to keep what happened to you alive in color and form. You are all experts in recording the history of your lives."

The people exchanged glances that betrayed their happiness at hearing these words being spoken. It was crystal clear now that they had not been wasting their time by coloring and recording their existence so diligently. This description of someone from outside their community did their lives justice. They made ready to leave to give these words of praise a place of honor in their life's work, but the stranger motioned them to stay. Expecting more acclamation they remained where they were. The stranger gave them a kind look and continued:

"I am aware of the countless dedicated hours that you have spent on the composition of your stained glass windows. You do not rest until each part has exactly the right color and shape that expresses what you have experienced. Then you place this in precisely the right spot within the whole of your life story. Day in, day out in this way you labor to perfect this piece of art that is a rendition of your life. And thus the window becomes your life."

Without being aware of it the people straightened their backs while the stranger spoke. They lifted their chins just a bit higher and proud there they stood. Proud of their dedication, moved by the understanding that the stranger displayed of their life's work. More than one felt a lump in the throat, some wiped away tears.

The stranger was well aware of what happened. He smiled and said: "Every human without exception yearns to be seen. That is why we make narratives of what happens to us and how we experience what we go through. Thus, our life experience constitutes a part of who we have become and who we have always been. More than most you are aware of what the representations in your stained glass windows express. But there is a question that I would like to pose to you and that is this one: What makes your stained glass window come to life?"

Somewhat insecure the people looked either at their feet or high into the sky. Yes, they had felt seen by the observations of the stranger who had listened so attentively and had asked clarifying questions. This had made them glean even more meaning in their own windows than they had before. But those questions had been different from the one the stranger put to them now. "What makes my stained glass window come to life?" They wondered, bewildered. This question they had not considered before. They had been so immersed in their trade of producing narratives that hardly any time was left to deepen their knowledge of anything else than what had a direct relation to the work at hand.

A few people prepared to leave. The time they wasted here could be put to infinite better use in the perfection of their window. They could produce a colorful piece of the recognition they had been given, surrounded by a dark border signifying the disappointment they felt right now. Then if the sun would shine through this part of the window, the acknowledgment would lighten up while the heavy border intimated that this praise was a one-time occurrence.

"Wait a moment," one of them who had already stepped out of the crowd suddenly said. "I was just imagining how it would be if the sun shone through the piece that expresses what I experience here today. I know the answer to your question, even though I have never considered this before. It is plain and clear, absolutely obvious, as fresh as the dawn. It is the light that makes our windows come to life."

The stranger looked at the person speaking, nodded and so invited them to continue the exploration. The others trained their ears on the conversation in the middle and those who were halfway home hurriedly turned back, now they saw that all were mesmerized by what was being deliberated. The one who had spontaneously spoken searched for words to express the insight gained. "Just start at the beginning," the stranger advised. "What happens when the light falls through your stained glass window?"

"When the outside light falls through my window, I see all I have been through come to life again. All my memories of childhood and youth resurface, my broken heart, my happiness, my disappointments and victories. When the sun shines through my window, I see the richness of my existence come to life in front of my eyes."

"Well spoken," said the stranger. A quick look around showed that all were nodding their agreement. Many hummed the way people do when they are in accordance with what is being said. No one made any movement to depart now. The stranger asked a next question:

"What happens to you when you see your experiences come to life in this way?"

The person was momentarily silent, apparently not fully sure where to start. "We, of course, are aware that the sun shines most easily through the parts of light coloring," the human then started courageously. The others nodded and this visibly strengthened the one in the middle. "Sometimes those parts draw my attention first and then I feel joyous and happy. I think of all the good times I have had. I feel deep gratitude for the many times that good fortune smiled upon me, that I felt loved and appreciated, that I was happy in the company of others."

At this the speaker sought eye contact with loved ones, neighbors and friends who each and all started to shine and smile. Everyone recognized what was being said. The speaker continued:

"At other times my attention is drawn to the dark spots. Then before I know it I am back in times that were hard, when I felt challenged and insecure, that I was frustrated and unhappy. Sometimes I feel the inclination to emphasize this spot, as I feel the whole weight of the grief I experienced then as if it was only yesterday."

Now the speaker looked around somewhat bashfully. This was not a subject usually addressed in this land. Did people want to hear this? The others looked back with eyes full of understanding and compassion. They knew intimately what he meant, that's what they silently said. The emotions of long ago and more recent times that they had reproduced in their stained glass windows sometimes just washed over you. You could relive joy again, but more than once it also came to pass that a seemingly small event in your younger years suddenly got hold of you. Before you knew it, seeing a certain space then made you think you were not good enough or you were an outsider who just did not belong. Another spot in the window could suddenly make you feel how easily you always adapted to other people's wishes so it became hard to remember your own wishes and joys. There were spots that symbolized the conviction that all would turn out well, once you had everything under control. Other parts of the window showed that you had once upon a time decided to be good and stick to the rules, even to the point that this was noticeable in your own window.

The people who for such a long time had been working on their windows with utmost dedication were intimate with the dangers their favorite pastime held. They were well aware of the force of attraction of living from the past. They had never discussed this openly, but this clearly was an experience common to all.

The nods and glances of recognition seemed to give the speaker heart to continue:

"My life resembles yours and yet it is different. We all have been through various life circumstances. Or you could say: we have experienced similar life events each in our own way. And yet ... ever since the stranger has come and moved amongst us, I for one have become more aware of the patterns in my own window and yours. The similarities are beginning to attract my attention. All of us have dark spots and light in our windows. Love is a thread that moves through all our lives: no matter whether this is love for one other or more, for work, for nature or something you are fond of doing. Who of us had not been considering how we would reproduce the acknowledgment of the stranger in our window?"

The people muttered recognition and laughed in an attempt to break the palpable tension.

"Each one of our windows is unique and yet out of all the occurrences and emotions depicted, I feel that all of us yearn to distill the same: who we truly are and how we can take our next step into the future."

The crowd gathered even closer around the stranger and the speaker in the middle. It was as if everything they had ever thought while they were working on their windows was suddenly openly exposed between them. Their deepest feelings that they had not been aware of up until that very moment had been articulated. That was thrilling – simultaneously scary and good. They murmured a bit among themselves, unintelligibly for each other but mutually reassuring at the same time. Some briefly squeezed the hand of a loved one or asked each other in eye contact: "Where is this going?" In the silence that had ensued it was apparent that all were deeply moved by what was transpiring amongst them. "I suddenly see you," someone whispered to another, "and not your window first and foremost."

"What happens when you look out through your window," the stranger asked quietly.

The people went even more silent to be able to hear what the answer would be.

"When I look out through my window," the person in the middle repeated, pondering the question. A murmur went through the crowd expressing wonder and surprise. "When I am bent on making my window, I don't really look outside," the one in the middle then resolutely spoke. The others let their approval be heard. "I am completely focused on my window and consider where the piece that reflects my most recent experience will come out best. Often I try multiple locations until I find the exact right spot where it fits in."

Again from the crowd an approving murmur rose up. The speaker took time to concentrate on the question raised. "If I picture myself looking out through my window, of course, the best parts to see through are those where the color is lightest. It is obvious that this does not give as clear a view as through a normal glass window. If I really want to see what goes on outside, it is best to look through a normal window. But now that I come to consider this, I realize that often I do look through my glass stained window, much more often than I was inclined to think when you first asked the question. Every day I am at it to add new pieces, rearrange the whole composition and get a new overall perspective. If I am in the thick of this and look up from that vantage point, I do look at the world outside through the colored lens of the bit that I happen to glance through."

The speaker fell silent and no one stirred. Even the wind lay low so the leaves of the trees didn't rustle, the birds stayed put and the cats and dogs pretended to sleep.

"Never before did I realize that by allotting so much time to my window I often look out through a colored lens. Only now do I become aware that by looking through a representation of my past, I oftentimes look very subjectively at what goes on now."

The speaker went quiet. The others frowned or looked ahead with a serious expression on their friendly faces, while they took this insight in. Some rubbed their eyes, others had inadvertently covered their mouths with their hands, a next one looked around without seeming to see anything much. The idea that by their assiduous work of perfecting their stained glass windows they would have a colored view of reality clearly needed time to sink in. There was time. All the time in the world. No one now felt they needed to be somewhere else than where they were.

The speaker sensed the exact right moment to continue thinking out loud. "When I look through my stained glass window, one could say that I do not observe but subserve. I look purely subjectively. What I see is not how something or someone is now: because I look through a part of the window that has the coloring of something that occurred in the past. I have represented it in my window with all the joy or sorrow that I felt at the time. And with the conclusions that I drew about myself and the role that I thought I needed to play in the world. As a child I couldn't really make sense of what happened around me and this led me to believe that I was the odd one out. But if I am honest and that is what I am right now," for a moment the speaker looked down, gathered courage, glanced at a trusted one and then admirably continued:

"that fear to be laughed at I see in details all over my window. And I probably am not alone in coloring bits in a way that is just slightly more favorable to myself than how things really were."

Again the people murmured. "And I probably am not alone in collecting evidence to show that I have become someone and making those events come out especially well. On the other hand sometimes I portray myself not the hero but rather the victim of what transpires. Then I use a darker coloring than reality might justify. In short, I am discovering how much I am given to subjectivity. I color everything that happens to me or in my immediate surroundings from my own point of view. So every time I look outside through my window, I view the present through my colored interpretation of the past. I don't observe, I subserve and that is quite a painful realization."

With questioning eyes the speaker who had gone out on a limb looked at the people who stood crowded together in a stunned silence. Did they recognize themselves in this description or were their experiences different? The unspoken question was answered with contact-full glances and thoughtful nods. Yes, this was what everyone who spent extensive time perfecting their stained glass window experienced. They themselves looked at the present through their own coloring of the past – they became conscious of this now.

"The deeply dark parts prohibit me from seeing the outside world at all," the speaker continued with renewed zest. "If I focus on the hard times in my life, I hardly see what happens around me and often I even don't really care. When I drown in my own misery, I am just not so open to others."

Again by making eye contact people assured the speaker that they were not alone in this. Facing one's own troubles prohibited interest for others. Your own darkness could blind you for what happened around you. Inwardly they all recognized this phenomenon.

"That was then and this is now," the central speaker continued falling from one discovery into the next. "If I keep looking at the world outside through the coloring of my past, then I will never truly observe. Then I will keep on seeing everything through the coloring that I once gave to what has occurred. What will allow me to come to true observation? How do I come to the point that I can see what happens now as it truly is?"

The stranger smiled and said: "I have a counter-question. Day by day you work to perfect the multicolored work of art that portrays your life. And so the window becomes your life. But we just saw that light is necessary to bring your window to life. The light of the sun that can shine in only parsimoniously through the darker parts of your window. And you yourself just said," for a moment the stranger looked the speaker straight in the eye, "that you can only observe through the parts that are clear, that have not been colored by your subjective interpretation. Is that so?" The stranger asked in general.

"That is so," the people nodded.

"How would it be?" The stranger started and allowed for a moment of silence, "how would it be if you did not any longer devote yourself to perfecting the coloring of your stained glass windows but rather to the clearing of them? How would you be able to see the world if you could look out without a filter? And vice versa, when you were able to let your own light shine without being filtered?"

This hit home. The people looked at one another and it was as if they saw each other in truth for the very first time; without the coloring of what happened once upon a time; without an interpretation, a judgment or subjective story that seemed to become more true every time it was told.

"I observe you," one said to another.

"I see you," the other gave back.

It did not take long for all of them to start to speak to one another. They looked at each other and saw who they were. The light of the one recognized the light of the other. In the contact time was forgotten. And by the time someone thought of thanking the stranger for the lightheaded way they could relate all of a sudden, this person had vanished.

Lightheaded Co-creation

"How would it be if you did not any longer devote yourself to perfecting the coloring of your stained glass windows but rather to the clearing of them? How would you be able to see the world if you could look out without a filter? And vice versa, when you were able to let your own light shine without being filtered?"

Those are the questions of the stranger. This fictional character points to the right spot. Who is occupied with stories from the past or for a hopeful future does not live in the now. Lightheaded living dictates that you be in the present, not allow yourself to be distracted by settling old scores or speculating about situations that for the most part will never come to pass.

As the light you can live co-creatively. With a light head you co-create every moment. Life does not run a fixed course. Every encounter is an invitation to see what wants to happen. The more lightheaded you are, the freer you are able to create the circumstances with others in which all can flourish. Everything that occurs, what someone says or does, is information that you can shine your light on. If you are not attached to what ought to happen, you can lightheadedly deal with what is. What needs to change will change once you connect with another as the light that you are. When you allow space for true contact, when you are lightheaded in the moment, you clear the way for creation itself to manifest. You co-create along.

Headed for Lightheadedness - Three Exercises

Lightheaded living requires practice. You need to have a certain alertness to alight your identification with your stories and make your home in the light that you have always been. Below are three helpful exercises.

1. Beware of telling stories

All great wisdom traditions say the same: nothing exists but this moment. And this one. And this one. In all kinds of ways this is the message they all repeatedly impart. Not because this is such a difficult statement. They keep offering various forms of the same message because of our tendency to forget.

Once I am fully present in the moment, I have no thoughts about what ought to happen and I can let arise. As soon as I come with a story, however entertaining, I disappear from the now. Just see if you can catch yourself at this when someone asks how you are. Are you really giving a reply or are you relating what happened to you the day before? How are you now? What is alive in you?

Step into the game. There is a big difference between playing tennis and talking about playing tennis, as a friend of mine is fond of saying. As far as I'm concerned, let's play. This means that we respond in the moment in full faith that we have all we need to keep the ball in the game. As long as we discuss playing tennis, we can brag about the beautiful backhand we played or speculate on tomorrow's game. You begin to participate only when you enter the court with your racket and balls.

You might be startled at the number of times that you will see yourself talking of tennis without ever putting one foot on the court. Be kind and compassionate to yourself, just like the stranger in the parable above who patiently asked questions and never passed judgment. Becoming conscious of how you disappear from the moment is the first step on the road to lightheaded living.

2. Be quiet

The contribution of silence cannot be overstated. Truth is that only when you halt, you can take a look at what is around you. Only when you keep quiet, you are able to listen fully. Bring your attention inwards. In yoga this practice is called

Pratyahara: bringing the attention, that through our senses is mostly outwardly directed to objects that peek our interest, back in. It is assumed by many that the eightfold path of yoga was described by the Indian scholar Patanjali as early as the 2nd century BC. The practice of pratyahara or the training yourself in withdrawing the senses from their external objects and living from the inside out, according to this scholar, brings watchfulness, detachment, inner peace and a more open and free state of spiritual awareness.

Everything that happens around us causes an avalanche of all kinds of inner reactions, interpretations, old emotions being rekindled, fear and hope that all vie for our attention. At least as much is going on in our inner worlds as is in the outer. When we take a moment to pause, we can watch this. We can see what is going on inside us without going along with it. Once the emotions have calmed down, when the thoughts evoked have evaporated like clouds before the sun, we can let our light shine again without restriction. The more we speak from silence, the more our confidence grows in what comes up in us. You come from a different place than when you more or less automatically react to what is being said.

Some people experience sudden enlightenment. For others this is an accumulative process. Every year after winter solstice the days grow longer. At first only by a few seconds of extra daylight. Soon these are minutes, then hours. This is also how it happens for many in the training of lightheaded life.

3. Bow for who you are

Lightheadedness is nothing like the fairytale 'And they lived happily ever after.' The light can all of a sudden be overshadowed. Then it is as if we are being caught by a large wave while we are surfing magnificently one moment and thrown on the beach without mercy the next. We are too busy or just not feeling so good anymore. We feel shame that we have left the light state of being.

In those moments especially, the inclination is to go back into a story; to talk about effortless lightheaded living and thus do a fruitless attempt at leaving the horrible here for the happy over there. Dare I face the fact that I am a human being who like everybody else is prey to fluctuating emotions that come and go? Am I able to embrace those fluctuations and not prefer the so-called good above the so-called not so good?

In Asia, I witnessed how people bowed 100,000 times before the Buddha, how they performed full-body prostrations. By bowing they demonstrate fundamental respect to the Buddha as one who realized the light. Making these prostrations counteracts arrogance and pride. We can make bowings like that inwardly. Especially when we feel de-light, it is advisable to bow for the fact that we do not live up to our own ideal image. Thus, you step down the pedestal that we had erected for our own ideal self.

Can we not make a story, a drama? Not judge ourselves or withdraw shamefacedly to a quiet corner somewhere, but with utter simplicity continue breathing and do what is ours to do? This we can, if we are capable of not wanting anything else than what is here now. That is the practice: handle the situation, however difficult, with a light head. Handle yourself, however different you are sometimes from who you'd like to be, with a light head. When you accept what is, you will notice that what is will naturally change.

When you bow for what is, your eyes will lighten up. You will notice how the corners of your mouth start to curl up, how your whole face relaxes. Only when you truly accept that there is no need for you to permanently be the strong one, the wise one, the one who brings the solution – only when you are ready to release the image of your ideal self and accept who you evidently are, you prove to be the eternally shining light itself.

Lightsource

We take nourishment from the sun
The source of light that brings all to life
Makes grow and flower
Scorches sometimes
In merciless rays
That show us color
The world in all its diversity
From dawn until dusk

At times in our lives
We meet such a sunny presence
Someone with a clear view
Positive, full of love, warmth
One with light in their eyes
Who speaks from the heart
Who is aware of the light
That we are
Our essence

Maybe it is you
Someone who embodies
Light living
Who in every circumstance
- or at least in most -
Can stay in contact
Does not separate in 'you' and 'me'
Resisting
The seductive 'I am good'
And 'you are bad'
By staying at home
In the source of light
The lightsource that you are

LIGHTHEARTED

light•heart•ed (līt'här'tĭd) adj.

1. Not being burdened by trouble, worry, or care; happy and carefree.

Proposal to thefreedictionary.com:

2. Happy in living one's own destiny beyond limiting concerns.

Y ou are a light that shines like no other. Living on the basis of this realization is what I call being lighthearted. As soon as you know yourself to be a light that is part of all light and yet unique, you know you have a part to play. Each time that you can connect as a light, beyond the wishes and vagaries of the personality, to the light in another, the big heart is beating. All over your body you will sense the life in your cells. Your heart opens wider. Your eyes want to see all that goes on. Life is yours to live.

In the state of lightheartedness we are eager to contribute to the whole. By being who we are and doing what is uniquely ours to do. And by being conscious from moment to moment of the source we tap from and the consequences of our words and deeds. Does what we do and say, think and feel promote lightness in the world?

We are each of us unique. The light breaks through you differently than through any other being. As such we all have something of our own to contribute to society that we shape and form anew continually. Your smile might give someone exactly the push they needed to come back to their good mood. Your friendly gesture might remind the next person how wonderful it is to be truly in contact.

Lightheartedness can make every moment special. In no time as a conscious practitioner of lighthearted living you will notice that you have more energy at your disposal. It is as if you walk downhill. You feel inspired as your motivation to contribute comes from within. You are powered by an on-board motor.

I am happy to take you on a journey in this chapter to the amazing area of your destiny; the meaning of your life. Not as the endpoint but rather as the point that is not a point from which you can act full of light and full of heart at all times.

The Curtain of the Critical Voice-over

Living your destiny is the most beautiful and therefore also one of the scariest things you can do. Suppose what you essentially have to offer is not welcome? That you get no response whatsoever from the outside world? Or even worse, that people throw you glances that let you know they think you are weird, peculiar. It will feel as if you happily hold out your hand and others walk by indifferently. Or, that is what we are given to think.

That is why we try to avoid these kinds of painful disappointments from an early age on. "You should never have done that," we berate ourselves when a gesture made in love was taken the wrong way – that time you drew a beautiful picture for your parents on the wallpaper, for instance. "Fool, you ought to know better. Now see what happens with your stupid action. You better learn. Because it will only give you trouble if you keep acting this way."

To protect yourself from disappointments and other painful experiences, an inner voice is born which will protect you against all dangers from now on. This voice is far from gentle. Speaking to ourselves we do not mince our words. To the contrary, we are tough when it comes to every mistake that we make. Have you done a good day's work, even then this voice can settle the score with you on one tiny little miss that no one else even noticed. You noticed it and inside you bust your chops. "You need to get your act together. You can't afford to let things slide. This way you'll never amount to anything. Pay attention to what you do," or similar words.

With such a severe inner dialogue we keep the Curtain of the Critical Voice-over tightly shut. Until the moment that you pull it open to allow your light to radiate fully again. This pulling open is easier than you might think. The six examples in this chapter will demonstrate how others became lighthearted by taking these three consecutive steps:

1. Begin to recognize your inner voice-over by the harsh tone, the you-form and the critical content

2. Bestow gratitude on your inner voice-over for its good intentions

3. Be brave and name your heart's desire and invite the voice to support you

Below you will meet Robin whose successful outer demeanor hides an inner world of self-reproach. You will see how he gains insight in the light that he essentially is and how he applies this. Then I expand on the dialogue with the critical voice-over that we all conduct within ourselves. I will show that the criticism with which you harass yourself actually points the way.

Precisely that which the voice warns you against doing the loudest is that what will prove to make your heart sing. This is where the danger of disappointment looms largest. You will see this demonstrated in the examples of people who, when through a process of asking just a few questions, come closer and closer to what fulfills them.

At the end of the chapter I shed light on the three steps indicated above so you yourself can start to make your life as meaningful to you as has always been the promise inside you.

Robin's Rambling

Robin is a businessman. Not someone who has much patience with himself or a psychological approach. Let alone spirituality.

"That is too difficult for me. That I leave to my wife who is the real clever one in our household," he says elegantly but dismissively. Yet we get into a conversation, because his marriage is bound to hit the rocks because of the inordinate amount of time he spends working.

I ask him how he speaks to himself about this issue that he cannot seem to tear himself away from the office or from the laptop when he is finally home where other people would love to have some of this attention.

"I carry a lot of responsibility for a big number of people," is how he starts. "That goes way beyond the life of privilege that my family can lead, thanks to my income. I cannot afford to let anything go pear-shaped. If I close my laptop by the end of the day, a huge unrest grips me. I often immediately open the thing again to check for mail. In other countries the day has only just begun when my wife and kids expect me home."

He falls silent for a moment. When I keep quiet as well, he continues:

"What an incredibly soft bastard you are, is what I think in those moments."

There is an edge of anger in his voice that wasn't there before.

"You would like to know what kinds of thought I have about my working hours that often extend into the night? Well, I will tell you what I think about that: Who is in charge here? Isn't that you, arsehole? Allow these people to get on with it and stop getting in their way. If you promise to come home on time in the morning and be part of family life, then do it! Just do it! What kind of a wreck are you that you can't get your act together? A pathetic, unreliable son-of-a-bitch is what you are! Playing boss during the day and then proving unable to be boss of your own time. Not making time for your family that you profess to love so much. You're able to close your computer, aren't you? You can trust the people who work for you, can't you? Why do you feel you have to be on top of everything? Do you really think the shit will hit the fan if you're not aware of all details? Angela is right. You have to learn to let go. But you can't. You just don't dare. What are you afraid of? Come on, close the laptop!"

He has noticed that I have been listening to him with utmost attention. I look at him and pose a question that he might not have expected: "And? Does it work. Do you then close your laptop and go home?"

Robin slides back in his chair. "I wish," he sighs. "No way. It doesn't work at all. Sometimes I sit in the office for hours wearing my coat. I just can't leave. I can't do it. Even if I call myself all the names in the dictionary, even when I push and pull to get myself to stop – I stay put. I know that I am putting my marriage at risk. I am well aware that I disappoint my kids time and again and yet, I don't go home. I wouldn't forgive myself if I missed something important. The buck stops with me, so I have to be aware of everything that goes on. You can't let anything slide, because you have the overview, especially in a company like ours. This is also what my father taught me: first in, last out. The times were different, of course. People can reach me day and night wherever I am but still – you can't allow for an opportunity to go unnoticed for want of paying attention. Then you'd be the one who lets the whole family business go down the drain."

I sit up straight when I hear his last sentence. "Who says this?" I ask.

"Who says what?" Robin responds with a tired voice.

"You said: 'Then you'd be the one who lets the whole family business go down the drain' – who said that?"

"I did, of course."

"Yes, I heard you. But what part of you?"

"What part of me? The part that expects me to do my work properly. The part that doesn't stop pointing out to me that I might not be up to this level of leadership. The part that tells me over and over again how many families depend on the decisions I take. That part!"

Robin has swallowed his parents. And thus he has sidelined his own light and become a toy of the inner voices that seem to be the ones in charge.

Ask kindly

In life often we come in without asking. We start a conversation without inquiring if the other person is open to this subject or our approach. In the realm of personal and spiritual development you can do this differently. Before you come straight to the point, first ask if this is a good time, if the other is ready to start the conversation. The same goes for talking to yourself. As this chapter shows there is no harm done in acting kinder towards yourself. The results of a kind approach might come as a surprise.

"Do you ever ask a colleague to do something they might not yet fully understand but that you know will render good results? I want to invite you to give thanks to the voice that is on your back for not going home on time. Out loud or else silently you might want to say something like: 'Thank you for reminding me that I am not only a workhorse, but also a father and a partner. Thank you for all the warnings you issue.' Do you think you can do that?"

"And you think that's helpful? " Robin asks incredulously.

"Fine," he then says. He breathes in a few times and closes his eyes. This is how he sits for a few minutes in the chair opposite me. I keep my heart open and let my light connect to his light. When he opens his eyes, I suddenly see how deeply blue they are.

Robin grips his chin. "That is a strange experience. When I did as you suggested, I had no expectation whatsoever. But as soon as I started thanking the voice, all of a sudden I saw my mother. My parents split up, because my father spent more and more time at the office. The words I use to herd myself home are almost literally the same ones my mother used to hurl reproaches at my dad. 'During the day you play boss, but meanwhile you have no say over your own time' – that is what she used to tell him if he came home late again. It did not work for my father and it doesn't for me. But thanking this voice was helpful, for one way or another I have a sense that this voice now feels heard. That my mother feels heard, while she speaks in me." He strokes his chin. "My mother speaking in me – it's a good thing no one gets to hear the nonsense I talk in here."

There is another voice that wants to be heard and thanked. "You stay at the office because you cannot afford to miss opportunities. You will not be the one who lets the family business go down the drain, you say. Can you show your gratitude to that voice as well?"

Without protest he follows my proposed course of action. But now he opens his eyes only after a short while.

"You're not going to tell me this is the voice of my father, are you?"

And when I nod, he curses softly. I do not need to know what has transpired between him and his father or what goes on in him right now. I see him in the light and thus help him find new ground.

"Just thank this voice for its concern. This voice reminds you of the load you have taken on by stepping into the family business. Just see what happens when you show gratitude to this voice that wants to make sure you don't let it slip through your fingers."

Robin closes his eyes again. He takes his time. Slowly I see a vague smile appear around his mouth. When he looks at me again, he says:

"I feel like an empty cathedral. One in which the sunlight streams through the windows high up. That is quite a difference with the sense that my head is like a chaotic court of justice in which clever lawyers state their cases. I haven't felt this peaceful in a long, long time."

There is one more step to go. "In that quiet space … from that quiet space … how do you want to divide the time between work and home? Just see if you can stay in touch with your feelings, the feeling of being an empty cathedral. That you yourself are the space in which your life is being lived. Place your intention in this space, your wording of how you feel you serve your roles of head of your family and of your company best. Then contact those voices again that you know so well and ask them to support you in manifesting this intention."

We sit quietly together for a bit once we are done. There is nothing to say. We smile at each other. As if we share a secret. As if the veils between us have lifted. All curtains are open and we can look inside one another just like that.

Thank instead of Fight

Robin has tried everything. He obeyed the voice of his inner critic. That didn't work well for him. When he conceded to this voice that told him to stay at the office to make sure no opportunity for the company would be missed, he got an earful because he didn't go home. When he listened to the voice that told him he was a softie if he didn't dare leave the work to his employees, he was reminded that he might well be the one responsible for letting the company go down the tubes. Left or right. Whatever he chose, the critical voice-over got the better of him.

He tried to silence the voice by coming with counter-arguments. To no avail. Whatever he said, the voice always came back with new arguments. The harsh inner voice always had the last word. It was simply impossible for him to win. But by thanking the voice instead of fighting it, he found space to look at the way he himself wants to direct the course of his life.

Although the inner critic tends to talk to us in a highly unpleasant tone, there is ample reason to thank this voice. Remember that the inner voice has arisen to protect us. One could say that the voice – this part of ourselves – has taken this task very seriously. So seriously that it seems as if this voice wants to keep you sound and safe on the same square foot where you already are. If you stay where you are, nothing bad can happen to you. As long as you don't take risks, you will not get hurt. The problem with this solution is that the voice isn't happy either when you stay home to sit on the couch. Then it reminds you in not too sweet a way that everyone is getting on with their lives and that it will not take long for you to fall behind.

It seems as if there is no remedy against this inner critical voice-over. But there is. Do not listen to the harsh words and the stern comments but to the underlying intention of concern. That is step one. The gruff inner commentator wants nothing less than keeping you out of harm's way, protect you against disappointment and failure, make sure you remain undamaged and intact. Thanking the voice for its concern is the key to lighthearted living.

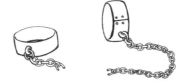

Swallowed Parents

By paying homage to the inner voice and giving thanks for its concern you pull the Curtain of the Critical Voice-over open. This brings you in touch again with the light that remained hidden behind it. In this chapter you learn to recognize this voice as what it is: the voice of a caring, worrying parent that you have, as it were, swallowed.

When you were small, it was the task of your parents and others involved in your upbringing to take care of you. You had to be fed and bathed, you had to get enough nourishment and sleep. You should not catch a cold, fall out of bed or get burnt in your bath. You had to learn to share your toys, to read and write, to take other people's wishes into account. All the time your parents are insecure whether they are doing OK. And afraid that in spite of their care something would still go wrong. It would break their hearts if something bad were to happen to you. If you were to fall ill or worse – perish the thought. "Watch it; you'll fall!" They call out when you take your first steps. They are proud of your accomplishment and at the same time they are terrified.

Most parents want the best for their children, but they don't always have the endless patience they would like to have. "Can't you ever do anything fast?" They might say and you are ashamed of being slow. "Why are you being clumsy again?" Is another one of those parental questions that just has no answer but leaves an impression. Or: "Where were you – don't you know we were waiting?" Once you focus on it, you see and hear lots of little comments that parents make on their children in passing:

☼ "No, you can't have a drink – you will just spill it."

☼ "Watch out that you don't hit anyone – you're always so wild."

☼ "You have to be the wise one now."

☼ "Now look at what you have done..."

☼ "How dare you ...?"

☼ "Would you please stop that?!"

☼ "I thought by now you knew that ..."

☼ "Aren't you old enough by now to know ..."

☼ "No, do not touch – what am I saying?!"

☼ "I want, I want ... I have a few things I want from you!"

☼ "OK, enough is enough!"

☼ "Yes, I heard you. You don't think I'm deaf, do you?"

☼ "Are you finally coming or what?"

☼ "So is this what you wanted?"

☼ "Can't you ever tidy up behind you?"

☼ "How often do I need to say that ..."

☼ "Are you unable to listen?"

☼ "Don't you see I'm doing something else?"

☼ "Can't you ever pay attention to another?"

☼ "Are you ever satisfied or what?"

☼ "You can do better, can't you – I expect more from you."

☼ "Can't I leave anything to you?"

☼ "You are a dear but, here, let me do it."

☼ "You are one spoiled brat."

☼ "If only you knew how many other children would be over the moon with this!"

☼ "What do you mean, no more money?"

☼ "Yes, cry! Don't think it will soften me up."

☼ "Go out. In those clothes. I don't think so."

☼ "Once you get some good marks, then we'll talk again."

Imperceptibly, bit by bit we have taken in these comments of our parents and other grown-ups we knew. All admonitions and reproaches, all their bidding and forbidding complete with the impatience and the anxious tone that parents display. Sigmund Freud, who was the first to describe this internalized outside world with all its standards, values and norms, called the resulting inner voice the superego. Dutch trans-personal psychologist Els Kikke one day called this phenomenon 'the parents we swallowed' and this term has stuck with me. Because this is what happened: we have so to speak swallowed our parents with all their words of warning.

Our parents are not to blame. They did all they could. Maybe they were still children themselves. They had a busy job, other children that claimed their attention as well, financial worries, stress in the relationship, insecurity about their role as a parent. Parents have not been given any special education and yet, they have to somehow get you ready to be able to stand on your own two legs one day.

And then there is that complex interaction between parents and children about setting boundaries and crossing them. It is the parents' task to set boundaries within which their children can grow in a healthy way. It is the children's prerogative to push the envelope. Boundaries, like norms and values, are not set in stone but change with the times. This play between age groups is the subject of countless songs such as this one from my younger years by Yusuf Islam who then was still known as Cat Stevens:

It's not time to make a change
Just sit down and take it slowly
You're still young that's your fault
There's so much you have to go through
Find a girl, settle down
If you want, you can marry
Look at me, I am old
But I'm happy

All the times that I've cried
Keeping all the things I knew inside
It's hard, but it's harder
To ignore it
If they were right I'd agree
But it's them they know, not me
Now there's a way and I know
That I have to go away
I know I have to go

Each child has their own way to go to become the adult that has been inside her or him from the beginning. But the admonitions we get to hear in our childhood still sound long after. Inside we remind ourselves as grown-ups that we have to perform and behave in all kinds of ways that help us stay safe and well. In the meantime life asks of us that we grow and become who we can be. Below I describe three ways in which you can start to recognize the inner critical voice or your swallowed parents. Once you realize that it is the intention of this voice to protect you, you can calm this inner voice down. You give thanks for its concern, for the endless efforts to keep you safe.

The examples show what kinds of questions you can ask – yourself or someone else – to get to the heart of the matter. When you express gratitude for the intention to keep you safe, you will feel how the Curtain of the Critical Voiceover dissolves. You will again come in touch with the light that wants to shine through you the way it does through nobody else. When you state what you want, what your next step is in realizing your destiny, you can ask your swallowed parents for their support. In the stories I tell you will see what this process gives them: space, air, lightheartedness.

Recognizing the Critical Voice-over

There are three clear characteristics that make it easy to recognize the Critical Voice-over:

1. The harsh tone and content

The critical voice-over sounds stern, angry, gruff and harsh. Some people have gotten so used to talking to themselves like this that they don't even notice anymore how mercilessly they attack themselves. The voice might also sound tired, endlessly tired. As if what is being said has been said thousands of times with no result whatsoever. It evokes the image of surly head shakes, you hear the heavy sigh of all futile efforts.

The content of the words isn't very merry either. If it is not an exhortation to get you moving, it's a reproach because you're moving too fast. Once upon a time expectations of you were high but it will all amount to nothing. You're a basket case. That's what it all boils down to.

The voice is not wary of exaggeration. When once you are late, the voice wonders why you are *never* on time. When you have forgotten an appointment, it reminds you that you are a dreamer, *always* somewhere else with your thoughts.

2. The you-form

The critical voice-over can also be recognized by the you-form in which it speaks. You talk to yourself just like a parent talks to a stubborn child. "Can't you watch out?" You scold yourself when you stumble with a cup of coffee on your first day on a new job. You weren't too sure of yourself to begin with, and being talked to like this by yourself doesn't add to your self-confidence. "Could you not have foreseen this?" You rebuke yourself when it turns out that there is no space left at the popular place where you have agreed to meet with someone you like. "So there you are then," is all the voice can contribute to your panic when you have no idea where else to go. Just notice how often you can catch yourself at talking to yourself in this you-form instead of the "I" that you are.

3. The relentless argumentation

The critical voice-over wants to have the last word and often has it, too. You should be different than you are: better, smarter, more adapted, better dressed, easier to get along with. If you go left, this voice will tell you that right would have been better. If you go right, the voice will keep asking you why in heaven's name you didn't go left. Whatever you do, the voice is impossible to please. It can always find something to hold against you. When you come up with an answer to the reproaches in your direction, this voice will find numerous ways to prove you wrong again. There is no end to its arguments that prove that whatever you do or don't do, you never get it right.

Beyond Self-doubt

"I think I can achieve more but I am scared." This is how Susana summarizes her predicament. She has always assumed she wasn't smart enough to continue her education. After high-school she got a job. But she now experiences an itch. Maybe she still wants to take a training that opens up more opportunities for her. But as soon as she considers this, an inner voice berates her that she herself calls the 'head mistress'.

"What does this head mistress say about your plan to take a training?"

Susana need not think long to be able to reproduce her inner voice:

"If you do something, you need to do it well. At this age if you are still considering a training, you need to aim high, of course. You must do something that will give you perspective. It is no use studying a subject that doesn't get you a better job. Why not study law. Or economics. That gives you a broad base. It will be extra hard since you haven't studied for so many years, but at least your work experience gives you a head start on 18-year old college kids."

Susana's inner head mistress raises the bar. Is this what she herself had in mind? That is a question she cannot answer straight away. As long as the head mistress has such a strong say in the matter, the Curtain of the Critical Voice-over is closed. Only after opening that will she be able to access her own light.

Until that time she is at the mercy of the stern inner voice that seems to know right from wrong so faultlessly. It will keep at her telling her what to do and what not to do.

Acknowledge first

The swallowed parents in our heads want to be heard. As long as we ignore or fight them, they remain strong and will keep coming back to us with their discouraging statements and commands. As soon as we acknowledge what is being said by listening, they disappear into the background. Just think when you want to warn someone — you, too, want to make sure the other hears what you're saying. Subsequently, an adult is free to make their own choice.

The only way to calm the head mistress down is to listen to the intention that is hidden within the stern words.

"Can you see that the head mistress has your best interest at heart?"

"If she has, then she goes about it in a very dumb way," Susana says with passion. "To me it feels as if she wants to make me into someone I am not. I am not at all sure if I am up to an academic curriculum. I am also not sure if that is what I want."

She thinks for a moment and then says: "I have always been afraid to be a disappointment to my parents. Maybe it is time to let go of that fear. I, too, can see that the head mistress is a part of me that raises the bar so high that I cannot possibly comply. That no one can comply really." She laughs. "The head mistress always wants me to excel, to be top of the class. But in actual fact I am not the best at anything. I am just an average performer which is fine by me. I don't need to go to college. I never really wanted that. I prefer being creative. Let me tinker and I am happy. That is more the direction that I would like to pursue, even if that holds no job guarantees."

In one fell swoop the whole issue is crystal clear. The insecurity that Susana came in with has disappeared like snow before the sun. It turns out she knows very well what she wants. She does not expect herself to do the highest possible level of education. She doesn't have to prove anything. That gets rid of the high expectations put on her for choosing a direction for further schooling. Now she is free to explore.

"If you choose from the light that you are, what is it you want to do?"

"To be honest, I would love to train myself in the arts. Something creative. The head mistress is right in saying that I am not a bookworm. I am primarily a visually oriented person. Friends always ask me for advice after moving house. I just know where to place the couch so it looks good and the space is used optimally. I would like to do more with that. Not an academic degree, but a vocational training. Nothing high-brow, but something in line with what I tend to do and love anyway." She looks radiant.

"Would you like to thank the head mistress for her concern and ask for her support in this plan?"

Susana twists in her chair and then closes her eyes. Inwardly she says what she has to say. When she opens her eyes again, she is initially silent. Then she says: "Actually, it was very beautiful to thank the head mistress. I saw her right in front of me. And I went and stood right before her, looked her in the eye and told her how much I appreciated that she had been looking out for me. She looked back and all of a sudden all I saw in her eyes was love. Then she vanished. She just dissolved. And I felt all of this love inside myself. I feel that she is within me – while I have always considered her as an outside agent who wanted me to be someone I was not. So then I asked myself for support. I felt a big wave of love wash through me. As if I finally felt that I am good. That what I can do has value, too. And all this thanks to the head mistress – who would have thought?"

Susana is no longer prey to self-doubt. The way that her inner head mistress wanted to push her towards a university degree must stem from her background. Once she had thanked the inner voice, she could verbalize what she herself wanted. This is how step by step she finds the heart of what matters to her.

Running by Desire

I cannot tell you how many times I have invoked the discipline to exercise for just ten minutes every day. In this I believe I am no different than the next person. The content of your intentions might differ from mine but don't we all do it – don't we all believe that this time we will really have the discipline to eat or work less, to exercise or meditate more, to be kinder and more forgiving, to visit elderly relatives more regularly? What wonderful people we could be, if only we had the discipline. That is what I thought, until my research in the field of the swallowed parents gave me new insight. Isaac provides the perfect example of how this works.

"I don't know what's the matter with me," Isaac says, a civil servant. "I love to be fit. I want to do sports; running in particular. I have recently begun training again, but on my way home from work I can't stop myself from buying bars and stuffing them in. Afterwards I feel so disgusted with myself that I pour myself a drink upon coming home. If I don't watch out, I drink a bottle a day while I do not want that at all as I won't get into shape. What is wrong with me? Is it a lack of discipline?"

"What do you do to yourself about this?"

"Gutless bastard! Wimp! Display some discipline, would you? Ah, but you've never really had that. You just do as you please. One minute you want to run the marathon and the next you fall for something sweet. Make up your mind. What do you want?"

There are no two ways about this: it is the inner critic that tries to get Isaac in line. The result is the opposite. The harder he is on himself for lacking discipline, the worse he feels and the more chocolate he stuffs himself with. That's the cycle he is caught in. The only way out is to honor the critical voice-over for its concern. Not that Isaac's inner voice sounds in the least concerned. Yet this voice, too, stems from the impulse to protect. Isaac is a father himself so when I share the story of how parents would go to any lengths to shield their offspring from harm, he knows what I am on about: "I hear myself say the exact same things to my kids that my parents said to me. While, of course, I had vowed never ever to let that happen to me. But that's what all my friends say."

I propose to Isaac that we don't try and find the benign intention of his malicious sounding inner voice. We just assume that intention is there.

"Are you able to thank your critical voice-over for the attempts to save you from harm?"

In his job he presumably has had to thank people (with whom he had not had much interaction) for years of good service. In such cases he must have come up with kind words so people could leave on a good note. He laughs and raises his hand as a sign that he has gotten the message. He withdraws deep in his chair and folds his hands. After just a few minutes he looks at me again. "Done," he says with a happy smile.

Focus on the future

When you want to assist yourself or another to discover the light beyond the concerns of your swallowed parents, then focus on the future. Nothing is easier than to lose yourself in analysis of how things have come about. The past is full of occurrences and stories, while the future lies ahead of us unformed. There is not so much to say about this yet. The only thing you need to do is make sure you are open for what wants to emerge. This is also the focus of your conversation.

"Speaking from the space you feel now, how would you voice what you want?"

Isaac sits on the tip of his chair now. He gives me a penetrating look and says: "You know – this is not at all about discipline. This is not about one part of me telling another part what to do. Now I have paid homage to what you call the swallowed parents, I feel my own desire to be fit and healthy. I can't wait to get into my running gear. If I run from this point – it is no point but what the heck – if I run from this point, then I run without effort. I just know that is true. I feel my passion. Not only for running – for my work, for my wife, my family. If I now imagine I stuff myself with chocolate and then drown my sense of guilt in alcohol, it makes me sick. So this is not about discipline … Once I find my heart's desire, I run naturally."

I couldn't have phrased it better. This turn-around, from fighting the critical voice-over to thanking the voice for its good intentions, works magic. Once you plug into your own heart's desire, you will move. Light is not static. It is held back by walls, doors and curtains. But once you clear the way, it bursts forth.

Working from Faith

While she cuts my hair, Sharon always has a good story to tell. This time she relates of an incident with her landlord, who through the years has become a friend. Over dinner one night she had given him an insight into how well her business was doing.

"Afterwards I felt so immensely stupid," she says. "When I got home, I kicked myself around."

We make eye contact in the mirror. "What did you say to yourself?" I ask. Sharon who doesn't need prompting:

"You again with your impulses, your bursts of spontaneity. Can't you keep your mouth shut? Now your landlord of all people knows the ins and outs of your business. That's useful when he wants to raise the rent. When will you learn to keep silent? You've always been way too talkative. You still are. When will you learn not to go around telling everyone everything? You're running a business, not a circle of friends. When will you finally learn how things go in the grown-up world?"

She laughs heartily. "Well, you know how it goes," she continues. "I gave myself a hard time. Like I do now and then. I'm good at it. But this time something happened that I have never had before. All of a sudden I became angry. Angry with myself, or rather with that voice that is forever disapproving what I do, how I look, how I run my business, how I deal with clients. Suddenly I got mad and said to this voice: 'Enough now. Stop bossing me around!' How about that?"

I am all ears. Sharon gives me a triumphant look in the mirror and keeps me waiting a bit before continuing her story. "It worked like a charm," she then says. "Finally I got this voice silenced."

We are both quiet for a while. Then she says: "But not for long, of course. Are you familiar with this voice in your head that gives a running commentary on everything you do?"

While she concentrates on her work, I assure her that I am all too familiar with this voice. I add that synchronistically I am working on ways to silence this inner commentary voice. On the spot I ask her if she would be a guinea pig for the method I am developing.

"Try me," she says. "Anything to get rid of the bastard."

"Right. I will give you an assignment," I say while Sharon is combing my hair forward so it completely covers my face. Does she do this on purpose? By accident? I decide not to be bothered by it. "An assignment that you will do in silence and then you tell me what happened. OK?" I hear her laugh.

"As long as it is not anything my mother would not approve of, fine. Tell me what to do."

"The assignment consists of three parts. First you will thank the critical voice that you hear inside for its words of caution. If you are in the process of cutting around my ear, you also caution me to sit still. It is very kind when someone wants to protect you from potential danger, even if you don't consider it very dangerous. That is one. In the meantime pay attention to your feelings. As a second step I invite you to tell the voice that you are no longer a child, but a capable grown woman who has been running this place successfully for years now. Gently let the voice know that for years you have been able to look out for yourself. And finally you ask the voice to have confidence in you, to be behind you and go along with the way you conduct business."

Sharon has stopped cutting my hair. Behind me I hear her breath deep. Then she says: "OK, if you say so. In short: thank, notice how I feel, make it plain I have grown up and ask for confidence in my way. Four elements if I count well, but fine. How long should this take?"

I give my standard answer: "As long as it takes."

After a couple of minutes at most she combs my hair back. "That's a super trick," she exclaims. "That really helps. I feel like I have always been pushing against some force and now I have the wind in my back. I really felt the voice change when I gave thanks for the cautioning. It was as if it first grew bigger from some kind of pride and then disappeared like a genie in his bottle. I had to hurry to ask that I can look out for myself and ask for backing me up. That's how fast this energy dissolved. And you know what's weird: I am convinced that I can trust my landlord. He is a good guy. I don't doubt that for one second. Those concerns come from others, from people who are mistrustful. I am not. I think it is possible to do business on the basis of trust and I have always been the better for it."

She grabbed her scissors and works fast now. We don't speak much in the time I am still in her chair; but when our eyes meet in the mirror, the big smile on our faces says it all.]

Self-reflection vs self-criticism

"What have I done well and what could be better?" Those are excellent questions to ponder at the end of the day; in the commuter train on your way home, with a glass of wine or in a conversation with your partner. In such an instant you can hold your behavior against the light. That is self-reflection: to take a look at your own ways of doing with an open mind and without judgment. Quietly you view the day, what you did and did not do and you see where you can learn and improve. Celebrate how far you have come already and accept that you are not yet as perfect as you might want to be.

This puts self-reflection in a different category than the self-criticism that comes to you by way of the critical voice-over. This voice points you mainly to where you have gone wrong, what of course you should never have undertaken, what you of course should have omitted and where you ought to know better.

In doing so the critical voice-over sounds somewhat outdated. Old-fashioned in the sense that it looks like this voice is still a believer of the idea that scolding, blaming and reproaches will shape you up. Theories on how to raise children have changed a lot these past years. Corporal punishments that were the norm in the olden days have now been abolished far and wide. Many modern day parents opt for a coaching approach. They teach their offspring how they can handle difficult situations, how they can find solutions to their life questions. They show them there are always more ways than one to get over a disappointment or reach a goal. Thus they lay the fundamentals for the capacity of their children to reflect about themselves and the way they act in the world.

Those who have not been given this kind of education can learn this skill later in life. The voice of the inner critic is an excellent starting point as the swallowed parents often point exactly to a sore spot. Thank them for enlightening you on where you can improve and contemplate this. Without judgment or self-blame, but as a professor who studies the behavior of animals: "Hmm, interesting."

Life is one big experiment. No one knows exactly how it goes. We find out who we are on the way and what it is we have to offer. Self-blame doesn't add anything. With self-reflection you come a long way.

Rest in Peace

Now that he is terminally ill, Donald blames himself for his unhealthy lifestyle. He was twelve when he started smoking and for years he has been a heavy drinker as well. "How could I have been such a fool?" Is the rhetorical question he torments himself with now.

He is in a dark mood when I come to visit. I ask if he wants to talk. He doesn't. Or maybe he does. He shakes his head.

"It's all no use now."

I disagree. "Of course, it is still good to come to terms with your life as you have lived it. You want to rest in peace, don't you? That doesn't only refer to the physical body – it seems to me that to be in peace with yourself is an integral part of that."

He doesn't cut me off, so I persist.

"Would you share with me what you say to yourself about the way that you have lived?"

"Did you really not know you were poisoning yourself? Don't make me laugh. Yeah, maybe not when you were twelve. Duh. That is over fifty years ago by now. You have read a paper in the meantime, haven't you? Don't try and fool me that you were not aware that you were signing your own death-warrant. And now all of a sudden you wish to live? While all these years you have been destructive, now you have regrets. How dare you? It makes me sick to the stomach. Please go and complain to another. You are dying and there is no one to blame but you. It is your fault and no one else's."

He looks at me: "Had enough?"

I nod. And swallow. And ask my next question:

"Can you imagine that this voice represents someone – or maybe more than one – whose heart breaks with the realization that they are going to miss you?"

"Who is going to miss me, I don't know," Donald mutters turning his face away from me. "I leave that to you once I am no longer around. I will miss you, but fortunately I will not be aware of it by then." His laugh cuts right through me.

"Your inner voice has unspeakably horrible things to say about you that do no one any good. Below the words I do, however, hear something else. I hear pain and grief about the fact that you will not be among us much longer. The voice then turns into a kind of friend who scolds you because he is bound to miss you awfully. Can you follow me?"

"How would it be if you acknowledged this angry inner voice as the one of a friend? When you thank the voice in that capacity for its expression of friendship and love, what would you say to this voice inwardly in that case?"

Donald takes my hand in his. We both have tears running down our cheeks. "I am so dreadfully sorry to all the people who love me," he says. "I am so sorry that I am going to split. Wow, that hurts."

With the power still in him he squeezes my hand. Softly I ask him to admit the pain, to feel what wants to be felt. Together in this way, for minutes we sit in the eye of the storm. A storm that always passes. Donald lets go of my hand, wipes his eyes with his sleeve and sighs:

"It is the way it is. I have done what I have done." And then with a wry smile: "What can I tell you? I loved my life."

And so we sit for a bit. We chat about everything and nothing. What we say doesn't matter. Words are not important when you know yourselves to be the light.

Finding your Feet

Not for a minute do I underestimate how hard it can be to be young. While you do not yet have a clear sense of who you are, you have to go out, get educated and make a living for yourself. And not only that, there is this persistent image of youth as being carefree, happy and successful. If you move in circles where this is the norm, you are bound to feel a loser if you don't really know how to do that: find your destiny, land a job that you love or a partner you can share your life with.

I see many young people who are somewhat ashamed that they don't know how to do these things that their mind tells them should be easy. Some of them take fright when I share that it took me almost forty years to find my feet. Others are hugely reassured by the idea that they are not the only ones groping in the dark. And of course, I always tell them that I would not feel as rich as I do if I had been able to make a beeline to my destination. I could not do what I do now without the learnings of my younger years. They look at my gray hair and we speak of the things they find hard to admit to themselves; things they think they ought to be able to do just naturally. I tell them they underestimate life, like I used to do, and overestimate themselves. No one is supposed to be able to be a star at a relationship or a job just like that. We're only human. The idea is to find joy in the discovery. And to go the way is in small steps.

Esther's predicament is a classic case of someone who is at the mercy of swallowed parents with unrealistically high expectations that argue over her head. Small steps towards her goal give her breathing space and much needed self-confidence.

Half a year ago Esther quit her job to start her own practice coaching people out of behavior that leads to obesity.

"Everything I have tried has failed," she says. "I should go out and find myself a job again because this is never going to work."

Is Esther in self-reflection or self-criticism? Her beaten down demeanor and use of the word 'never' point to the latter. It sounds to me that she might be unrealistic about what it takes to set up your own practice. Of course, she will succeed. But not if she is this defeated. To build a clientele, she will have to work from the light that she is.

"What do you say about this to yourself?"

Esther sips from her herbal tea and says: "I had expected more of myself. I thought I could do it. Now I see how stupid that was. I had a few ideas to get started and none of them worked out. It is as if no one wants me. It is as if I have been dreaming. And dreaming gets you nowhere as is plain to see now."

"What do you say to yourself? Do you have an inner voice that berates you on this and if so, what does this voice tell you?"

"Oh, that's what you mean," Esther says. "Yes, that voice I know only too well. That one says: 'You should have had a flourishing practice by now. It's not a lack of talent. I can't understand why you don't have more clients. Don't they see how good you are at what you do? How come? You should have had a site. It's a shame you still haven't got one. Is that the reason people don't get that they should come to you – because you don't promote yourself. Why don't you get out there and sell your wares? What's wrong with you?' Is this what you mean?"

Like me you will by now see what we are dealing with: swallowed parents who are having a conversation about Esther. The one parent argues how good and wonderful she is while the other is convinced that she ought to work harder at marketing herself. Thus these swallowed parents resemble the archetypal father who wants to toughen the child up to make it able to negotiate the world, and the archetypal mother who glosses over the behavior of the child. The child is caught in between the two and remains a child. Growing up happens in spurts. Esther is well poised to make a jump ahead now.

"This voice clearly wants the best for you, but you are more than just this voice. How would it be if you thanked this voice for its engagement in your life?"

"Thank it …," she says indecisively. Only to continue out loud: "Dear voice, I hear what you say. You have a lot of confidence in me, maybe too much."

"Concentrate on thanking the voice," I remind her.

She starts again. "You have a lot of confidence in me and I want to thank you for that. To be honest, I only now begin to appreciate how good it feels that you hold me in such high esteem. So, again: thank you. And thanks, too, for the suggestions of what I can do to build my practice. I had thought of them myself, but it is always wonderful to find someone who cares about me, so thank you."

Before my very eyes Esther has transformed by what she herself has said. She is sitting up straight now, the handkerchief she was fumbling with a moment ago now forgotten on her lap.

"It works!" Is her comment. "I feel as if I can move again. I've been so stuck and I kept thinking the same over and over again. Hundreds of times."

I assure her that she is not the only one plagued by recurring thoughts, especially when doing something for the first time with no guarantee of success. In those circumstances the swallowed parents arise in full force. How would it be if Esther could harness this power?

Falling off your pedestal

Working with your light implies that you let go of images of who you are or could be. Without being aware of it we often attempt to project an ideal image of ourselves. The world should remain unawares that we aren't perfect. Sometimes we don't even want to confess this to ourselves. To face everything includes that these idealized images are to be shattered. Allow yourself to fall off your pedestal. It hurts for an instant, but then you will notice what a relief it is to not have to keep that image up. All the energy that is now at your disposal. Available in the now.

"You could make a next step by formulating what it is that makes your heart sing and ask the voice to get behind you. Can you find the words?"

Esther clutches her hankie again and starts to fumble. So I suggest that she returns to the practice of gratitude and just looks at what emerges in the space that comes from the swallowed parents retreating. "I wish to give myself the chance to try this for a whole year," she then says calmly. "I know that I need to work on my site. The strange thing is that I now am in touch again with why I wanted my own practice in the first place. I thought I had to have a full list of clients right away, but that is probably not how it goes. I want only to be happy with the clients that I have and build up from there." I remind her that she can ask her swallowed parents for support.

"Would you help me?" She simply asks. She is momentarily quiet and then says: "When I was small my mother used to lay her hand on the small of my back. It feels warm now in that exact same spot. As if someone is behind me. As if I am behind myself."

Daring to Love

Confused is too weak a term for the state Joey is in. He is discombobulated. On a recent training he slept with a fellow trainee, while his girlfriend is expecting his child and wants to move in with him.

"Are you able to give me a brief impression of what you tell yourself about the situation you find yourself in?"

"I'm kicking myself around," he says.

"Let me hear what you say, without giving me the details."

He commences: "You arsehole. Is this what you want? That you cannot face Lucille while she expects your baby? And you want to become a father? What kind of a father are you when you can't handle yourself? That is not the kind of father a child needs. It is better off without you. F… off. You can't look that child in the eye. Who can trust you now? Lucille certainly won't and right she is. You can't trust yourself. You are just like your father!"

Joey has avoided looking at me while he spoke. He doesn't mince his words which I appreciate. Let's get real here.

Follow the voice

The Critical Voice-over and the swallowed parents try with all their might to protect us from what can go wrong. When you pay attention to what they say, this gives you the clue to what you yourself would like to see happen. Precisely that what makes your heart skip a beat is what the voice seems to fear the most. Afraid that you will be disappointed, the voice tries to keep you from it. The Curtain of the Critical Voice-over is pulled shut tightest at the place where your true passion resides.

I discuss with Joey the difference between having regrets and blaming yourself. Joey is deeply sorry for his impulsive action. He wished he could undo what he did. Regret is a pain that must wear off. Also the acute pain that he has caused his partner Lucille will pass and they will have to work on restoring the confidence within their relationship. That's how it is. But Joey now suffers from a merciless inner critic who does not seem to want him to get away with this.

"Can you hear the concern that you might not be fit to be a father?"

"I feel very insecure about that," Joey confesses straight away. "I wasn't so sure of the whole thing and then Lucille was suddenly pregnant. I was pretty upset when she told me." He looks at me. "Do you think that's why…?"

"How would it be to thank the voice that gives you such a hard time for its anxiety about you becoming a father and concern for the child?"

Joey promptly stares ahead. His lips are moving and he frowns. Then I see him relax a little. He scratches his head and looks at me: "I am scared to death of becoming a father. My own dad left when I was little and I am so afraid that I will do likewise. I just want to care no end about that kid. But I am not sure if I can."

"Why don't you ask your inner critical voice-over to help you out?" I suggest. "You just ask for help in something that no person can be sure of. Invite the voice to support you in gaining self-confidence. Just see what happens."

Again Joey stares into the nothing far away with an earnest expression on his face. Then he closes his eyes. I see him nod. Once. And once more. As if he makes a promise. His eyes are clear when he opens them again.

"I have seen the light," he then says in jest and a bit shy. "I loved my father even if I hardly ever saw him. I have now asked the voice to help me to love myself just as much so I can fully love the kid. And Lucille. I will go on my knees for her. She can scold me all she wants but I will not leave. I want to raise this child with her. That's all I know."

Three Steps to Lighthearted Living

The meaning of your life is your life itself. Each instant that you follow what makes your heart sing is meaningful. It lifts the spirit. It allows your light to shine. It makes you spread lightheartedness. To be lighthearted we – you and me – need to stop letting ourselves be bullied by the voice of the inner critic. These three steps allow us to draw the Curtain of the Critical Voice-over open and shine our full light. The light that we have always been.

1. Begin to recognize your inner voice-over by the harsh tone, the you-form and the critical content.

Catch yourself when you talk to yourself harshly, scold or blame or even bully yourself. Chances are you are at the mercy of the Critical Voice-over. This is the voice that you have installed at a young age. You have made this voice up out of all the admonitions, warnings and commands you heard from your parents as you grew up. That is why I tend to call this voice the swallowed parents.

As you will have noticed by now, it is no use at all to try and argue with this inner voice. The voice will always find a counter-argument. You can put the time you spend trying to get on top of this voice to better use. You might let the critical comments wash over you but that doesn't result in true happiness. The art is to learn to listen between the words to what this harsh and angry sounding voice means.

A parent's heart breaks when something happens to one of their children. That is the last thing they want. Their first and foremost worry is that you remain unharmed. The same goes for your swallowed parents. Your safety is the true purpose of the relentless running commentary that you give yourself inwardly on whatever you do and say. Once you start to realize this is the case, the voice ceases to sound so stern and discouraging.

2. Bestow gratitude on your inner voice-over for its good intentions.

The way to have your swallowed parents work for you and not against you is: thank them deeply for their concern and care. You let your swallowed parents know that you have heard them. Whatever they say, you do not argue. You do not shrug your shoulders and let it come over you. You listen and thank them for their concern by inwardly saying something like: "Thank you so much for cautioning me. I truly appreciate that you let me feel how it would pain you if I were to come to harm. Thank you for your immense care for me. Thank you that you want me to navigate life safely. I thank you from the bottom of my heart for your unending concern, for your love, for the fact that you suffer if I am not well."

With time you will find it easier to thank the voice in your own words. When you hit the right note, you will immediately feel the force of the critical voice-over lessen. The energy with which you just gave yourself an earful retreats to the background. When the voice feels heard and honored, there is no further reason to keep addressing, cautioning or bullying you. You will find unknown inner peace once this voice that could drive you crazy keeps silent. You will feel how the light that was hidden behind the Curtain of the Critical Voice-over immediately becomes one with the light that you are. You will feel more power, more confidence in plotting your own course.

3. Be brave and name your heart's desire and invite the voice to support you.

In the quiet space that arises within you by thanking the voice, you can take a look at what makes your heart sing. You can find your direction, act and see what this brings you. Some people plot their future and then follow the path they've set. Others let the future form itself by taking small steps and seeing what appears to be showing forth. You will discover what your way is. You will have more energy at your disposal whatever you choose now that you don't lose precious time in a never-ending inner game for and against yourself. When you let your light shine freely, the meaning of your life becomes clear. Your heart will sing. A light tune. Now. And now. And now.

Daylight

Always
It is day somewhere
On this world
On this globe
That whizzes
Through the universe

The uni verse
The verse that we all sing

If it is not day here
And we rest
It is day there
On the other side
Where they work
Eat and enjoy
The light of day

Good day light
That always is

HINDLIGHT

To dance with life. To be lightfooted whatever life brings you and however it challenges you to move beyond what you thought you were capable of.

To live in the now. Not to be trapped in stories of the past that determine how you look at what is in front of you at the moment. Or be distracted by speculations of the future. Lightheaded living.

To fulfill your destiny. To do what makes your heart sing with all the energy and zest that you have and with a deep sense of inner peace. To be lighthearted.

My love, what else could you wish for?

To practice these three qualities brings happiness. Another kind of happiness than you might be used to. Not a personal happiness that depends on nice weather, a good buy or the appreciation of others. Living as the light that you already are brings a state of happiness that is autonomous. Some call it bliss.

You are a light, part of the one light. That is what you have always been. And the light shines on each and all in equal measure. Happiness or unhappiness – the light does not discern. And so a new way of life begins.

To end with the words of the great Indian master Sri Ramana Maharsi, words which have guided me while writing this book:

Concentrate on the seer and not the seen,

not on the objects,

but on the Light which reveals them.

Thank you

A book is a collaboration of many who will not all be aware of their contribution. I would like to express my gratitude to all the people who have come to me over the years with their questions. In every meeting my insight grew in the steps we can take to pitch our tents in the light that we already are.

For their direct contribution to this book I thank Emma Jansen for exploring with me what I had to write about light living; Cathelijne Schuitemaker who convinced me of the importance of this book for the younger generation: and Harm Saeijs of the Amsterdam bookstore Au Bout du Monde who challenged me to dig deeper.

The term 'painstake' in chapter 1 is a translation of the title of the seventh book of thriller author Charles den Tex. Transpersonal psychologist Els Kikke gave me the 'swallowed parents' who are the main characters in chapter 3. Both instantly gave me permission to use these terms when I asked for which I thank them deeply.

Daniëla Postma helped me as an editor to find the depth that I was looking for. Her excellent suggestions provided the coherence that made the text into a book. I am grateful to Mariet van der Vloed and Jos van Merendonk for the critical eyes with which they read the manuscript and fished out errors and typo's. Nina Schuitemaker I cannot thank enough for the loving and merciless precision with which she went through the final version. In the end nothing happens without Daniël Doornink of Merx Publishing. Thank you for the light way of working together. If anyone is lightfooted and lightheaded, it's you.

For the English version I am deeply grateful to Dustin DiPerna who he took an immediate liking to the book when I told him about it. May his publishing house flourish and bring the light of consciousness to many. He contacted Isioma Kasim in Nigeria to edit the English version. His light touch made it only better. And then he asked Angeliki Savvantoglou to illustrate. How wonderful for a word person to work with such a delightful and talented image maker. Thank you, too, to James Redenbaugh for the beautiful book design.

Of course, my deepest gratitude goes out to my partner Jos van Merendonk who finds it absolute nonsense that I thank him for the light that he is and that he brings into my life every day.